# Crowded in the Middle of Nowhere

Dr Bo Brock

ISBN: 0615971075
ISBN 13: 9780615971070
Library of Congress Control Number: 2014903073
Rare Bird, Iamesa, TX

Perspective is what makes us who we are. The way we process the information that is presented to us and react to it determines the way the rest of the world perceives us. It is this precept that fascinates me. Being a practicing veterinarian in a small town demands that I understand this concept.

# Crowded in the Middle of Nowhere

I left Clarendon, Texas, in January 1992 to start my own veterinary world in Lamesa, Texas. When I left, a fella there who was a large part of why I departed told me, "Lamesa, Texas, is in the middle of nowhere. You will never be an accomplished veterinarian there. You will be an outstanding horse vet in Lamesa, Texas, when pigs fly!"

I started to name this book *When Pigs Fly* but decided that that title might be a little misleading. So I called it *Crowded in the Middle of Nowhere*. It is the story of being a veterinarian on the edge of the earth and loving it. Crowded because....we have managed to accumulate over 25,000 clients in this place he called the "middle of no where".

When I came to Lamesa, the local paper asked me to write an article once a month about veterinary-related things. That is what happens in small towns in West Texas. I wrote the first couple of columns about things such as parvo in dogs and why you should get a Coggins test on your horse. No one read them. I decided on the third attempt to write something a little more humorous about being a rural veterinarian. This—yes, this—made all the difference.

As fate would have it, someone in Lamesa had a relative who was a veterinarian in a state far away. She decided to send the story to him. He liked it so much that he sent it to a veterinary magazine up North. They called me later and asked if I wrote that type of article often or if that one was the only one I had composed. I told them about the local paper gig, and the fella at the magazine said he would love to put one article a month in the journal.

I have been looking for the moments in life worth describing ever since. This book is a collection of some of those moments. My grandfather, Elmo Brown, instilled within me a perspective on looking at the world. I remember listening to him at the end of the day at the dinner table; he'd tell stories to my grandmother that he and I had lived through together during that day. I quickly realized that I was not paying enough attention to everyday life. This set me on a lifelong mission to discover how my grandfather, Papaw, perceived the world. I will be forever grateful to him for loving me and teaching me to look for the moments that are right in front of us every day.

I hope this book touches the extremes of your emotions. I hope you laugh; I hope you shed a tear or two; and I hope you discover how wonderfully blessed we all are to have friends that are animals and realize all the smiles they prompt.

Read it with a thrust.
Find the moments!

The cover: The "Rare Bird" that decorates the cover of this book was a drawing spawned in the second year of veterinary school as my best friend John Horn and I sat hour after hour listening to endless lectures. About forty hours a week we set in the same classroom, in the same chair, trying to keep our attention focused so we could learn how to be doctors. But sometimes it just didn't work and we would loose focus and start drawing pictures. On this particular day the professor kept calling every disease we were learning a "rare bird". I am telling you, when your brain is already full of information that is important, learning the rare birds is of absolutely no interest. When we lost interest, we played a game we called "add a picture". In the game, I would draw something like perhaps a head and pass the paper to him. He would then add a neck or a body and then pass it back to me. I would in tern add another part and pass it back. My notes from vet school are littered with hundreds of these pictures.

But on this day we composed the rare bird. The man kept saying it over and over and Horn finally asked me what a rare bird looked like. We drew the bird that is on the cover of this book, and I have been drawing it every since. If you ever come to Lamesa, Texas, I might just draw one on your arm. I draw them all the time on patients and clients. If you know me, you know the rare bird. It is my favorite.

# Section 1

## The Beginning

When it comes to the public...perception is reality.

Chuck Deyhle
1991

*one*

## Otis

# Otis

Otis was a type-B fat guy. You know the kind I am talking about; he wears his pants *below* the belly. The type-A fat guy wears them *above* the belly, and those pants usually have a zipper that is about twenty inches long. Guys know what I speak of here. If you are ever at a football game, peeing at half time, and you hear a zip that lasts about two seconds next to you at the urinal, you can bet it is a coat unzipping or one of these fat guys with a twenty-inch zipper.

At two days postgraduation, I was not the surest diagnostician who ever lived. This was my first case, my first day of work, and my first venture into actually being a real vet. I was driving to the ranch, going through the possible causes of the symptoms that the man had explained to me over the phone. Clarendon is at the mouth of Palo Duro Canyon and is rough country. I was going over the fifth cattle guard after the sixth turn when I saw Otis at the foot of a steep cliff. I had never met him before. He was an overly thick man who, I would learn, always smoked a huge cigar and had the vocabulary of a sailor.

"Where is she?" I asked, only to see him point up.

At the top of this fifteen-or-so-foot cliff was a small, flat spot where the cow had collapsed and lain down. We climbed up the side of this dry riverbed together, him huffing and puffing, and me wondering what the heck this cow could have wrong with her.

When we arrived, I saw this huge Shorthorn cow lying on her side and paddling her legs. She had been paddling so long that she had dug trenches with her legs in the shape of triangles. I began to feel the sweat roll down my neck as I pondered what in the world could have caused this.

Otis said, "What in the h--- could be wrong with that big ol' cow, young doctor?"

I had no idea. I just needed to stall for a while and collect my thoughts. So I told him I had to get something out of the pickup and slid back down the bank to the truck to think about it for a second. I decided the best thing to do was to get some blood and see if lab tests could help. With blood collection tubes in hand, I scurried back up the cliff to the side of the cow and her big, fat owner.

Much to my surprise, when I stuck the needle in the cow's vein, the blood came back chocolate brown. Wow! They had taught me about this in veterinary school. Nitrate poisoning from grazing the milo patch across the creek. And guess what? I actually knew what to do.

The trip down the cliff found me walking with a higher step and even a slight whistle. I picked up the antidote and once again scurried back up the cliff.

Otis was impressed with my confidence and even smiled for a second. "So how long till she gets up after you give her this stuff?" he asked.

To this question, I had no answer. The books don't tell you that kind of information; they just tell you what to do to treat the problem. You see, this is why they call it the *practice* of medicine, and at this particular moment, I was working on my very first cow. There are some things you just learn as you go.

So I just gave him the standard I-really-don't-know answer: "It varies from animal to animal."

I gave the bottle of medicine in the vein, and to my surprise, she hopped right up. In fact, she hopped up and looked pretty mad. She looked real mad. She looked at me, and then she looked at him, and I guess she decided that he looked easier to catch and softer to head butt because she went running at him with mean intentions.

I did the only thing that any valiant veterinarian could do in this situation: I ran down the hill and jumped into the back of my pickup. I thought Otis was right behind me, and the cow was right behind him, but he wasn't. She had him on that little cliff, and she was whoopin' him. At first, I was amazed at his agility. For a fat guy, he was putting some moves on this cow. But only for a while. You see, at first she was still a little uncoordinated and stiff from being down so long. That took about three or four charges to get over, and then she had her youthful athleticism back. On the fourth pass, she got him. She rolled him like a rubber ball to the cliff's edge, and then with one mighty shove, over he went. Good thing that dry creek bed sand is soft, because he landed on his shoulder, and I really think I saw him bend backward so far that his head touched his fanny.

"Are you OK?" I shouted from the safety of the truck bed.

"S--- no!" he screamed back at me.

"Well, you better get well quick," I said, "because she is coming down that cliff with a bad look in her eyes!"

At this, he jumped his three hundred–pound frame up out of the sand and started rushing toward me. It was hard to tell exactly, but it looked like the cow was going to get him before he got to the truck. I noticed that his stride was getting shorter as he approached me, but I wasn't sure why.

I screamed, "Run faster! She's catching ya!"

He was wide open and still hadn't lost his cigar. As luck would have it, he got to me before she got to him, but he was too tired to jump into the truck, and I wasn't strong enough to pull him in. Plus, in the heat of the chase, his normally crack-showing pants had slipped down to just above his knees, making it impossible for him to throw a leg up over the side of the truck. As I was reaching over him, trying to pull him in, I just grabbed anything I could get ahold of—which, in this case, turned out to by his giant, size-52 boxers. Basically, I was giving my very first client a semipower wedgie.

He looked at the cow and at me and then bent down to pull up his pants. This left only enough time to start running around the pickup to avoid being rammed by the now-full-speed cow. Once again, I was amazed at his speed. He managed to stay ahead of her as they made laps around the truck. Each time he came by, I would offer him my hand and tell him to jump for it. But each time he thought she was too close, and he would back out at the last second and go on another lap. Finally, at the hood of the pickup, on about the sixth lap, she caught him. His pants had come down again, and his stride was just too short to outrun her. He was taking about fifteen steps per yard there at the end, trying to avoid her rush. But it was to no avail. He rolled up into a big ball, and she bounced him around and through everything in sight. I jumped out of the truck and did the best rodeo clown imitation that I could. She was determined to roll him awhile before she came after me.

But as suddenly as she had come up from that dose of medicine, she just quit and strolled off. When I got to Otis, he was covered in stickers and cow doo-doo. His hat had been smushed flat. His shirt was torn in several places. His pants were down around his ankles, and his giant boxer shorts were full of dirt. He was cussing a blue streak, but he never lost his cigar, nor did it sustain any damage.

I learned a lot that day. First thing is, if you are a type-B fat guy and work with cattle, you had better have suspenders. Second thing is, when you got a cow down from nitrate poisoning, you had better head for the truck right after you give it the antidote. Third thing is, I gave my first actual client a wedgie. I somehow knew that day that this was going to be a great career. I am convinced there are some things you just can't learn in school.

*two*

Otis Epilogue

# Otis Epilogue

I was twelve years old when I determined I wanted to be a veterinarian. I have always considered myself lucky for that calling because I have seen so many talented people wrestle with what they want to do and finding something that interests them. But after the age of twelve, there was never any doubt for me.

It happened on a hot, early August evening, this moment that persuaded me to become an animal doctor. Lucy, the only sow that lived on our farm, was having babies. Let me tell you, this was a big deal to twelve-year-old Bo. I had fed and taken care of that sow every day that she had been alive. She may have been just a pig to most, but she was my four hundred-pound buddy.

Lucy spit out the first baby, and I was there to see it. I was amazed by the entire process and couldn't wait to see how many she had and to have a herd of piggies to take care of. The second one slid out, and I was more amazed than ever. I pulled the afterbirth off them and shook them around. They immediately got up and headed for some titty milk. I was just totally entranced by birth and all that it included.

But something went wrong on the third one. Lucy strained and grunted, pushed and moaned, lay down and got up...but nothing came out. I knew there had to be more than two. What in the world could be wrong? I ran into the house and got Papaw. I told him that Lucy was having babies, and the third one wouldn't come out.

Papaw ambled out to see if his young grandson had any idea of what was going on. He looked for a few minutes and made some of those "hmmmm" sounds that old men make when they are thinking. After a few minutes, I could tell he had concluded that I was right, and Lucy sure enough had a piggy stuck.

He went to the barn and came back with some slick substance that I had seen him use before when delivering calves. He smeared it all over his right arm and hunkered down behind Lucy. I watched her eyes get big as the old man's arm slid into her birth canal. It seemed like ages passed before he finally said what the problem was.

"That piggy is coming upside down and backward, Turdhead. I am gonna have to put a lot of pressure on it to get it out. It ain't gonna be pretty, so if you want to go in the house, now is the time to do it."

*No way!* There was no way I was leaving at that moment. I told him I was gonna be there no matter what; I could take it.

He went to work trying to reposition the piggy and get it out. It was a painstaking process, and I could see him wince every time she would have a contraction and smush his arm. He worked hard at it. The minutes passed, and I could see sweat building up on his forehead. I didn't know whether to feel sorrier for him or her as they both worked hard to bring life from inside her.

Finally, he got that rascal out. It was huge, way bigger than the first two, and dead. It was just another moment in my childhood that confirmed that my granddad was a hero. He could fix anything, as far as I was concerned, and this was simply proof of that assumption.

He pitched the dead piggy aside and told me to stay there and see what happened next. I wouldn't have left for anything, and the fact that he trusted me to be the sentinel just made me more determined to see it through to the end.

About fifteen minutes passed, and Lucy began pushing again. Nothing. Ten more minutes, and all sorts of juicy stuff came out, but no piggy. I ran back in and informed Papaw of the new developments.

What we saw when we returned to her pen absolutely floored me. Lucy had prolapsed her rectum and vagina pushing the next piggy out. It was the most awful thing I had ever seen. Papaw took in all in stride, like it was som'in' he saw every day.

He simply went back into the house and returned with some of Mamaw's thread and a tickin' needle. He pushed everything back in and sutured Lucy shut. He told me that she was gonna die and that I needed to make sure those two piggies sucked as much as they could before she passed on.

I just couldn't believe it. Why did she have to die? Was there just nothing on Earth that one could do to fix a prolapse? I was just not going to accept that my pig was gonna die because there was nothing a person could do to fix a birthing problem.

His prediction came true, of course. She died the next day and left me with two orphan piggies and a lot of questions. I decided then and there that I needed to learn to fix stuff like this. I was certain that Papaw could have done it if he only knew how. That conviction never left me.

You might be wondering how all this rambling has anything to do with a type-B fat guy named Otis. Well, it had everything to do with him.

Fourteen years had passed since I told Papaw I was gonna grow up and be a veterinarian so I could fix things like what had happened to Lucy. I was headed out to do just what I had promised him for the very first time, and it just so happened to be for a cigar-smoking, cussing cowboy on a dry creek bed near Clarendon, Texas.

I can vividly remember thinking about it as I drove the twenty miles to meet my first animal in need. I can remember the emotion of thinking I had finally made it and was a real doctor. I went through that vet school with a determination few others could muster because I was intent on fixing every sick animal I encountered for the next forty or so years.

And I actually fixed that cow. She certainly would have died if I hadn't come into her life. And I am really proud of that. But I still feel the irony of how that first animal tried to dismember her owner, and I have contemplated the significance of that irony every since.

I put the last sentence in the story of Otis because I realized that day that many of the things Papaw instilled in me while I grew up were more important to being a good veterinarian than all of the science that Texas A&M taught me in vet school. After twenty-four years of practice, I still believe that is true.

# Section 2

## Family

Always look for the obvious, Big Doctor. If you find something else, they will name it after you.

Chuck Deyhle
1990

# Moment 1

### *Ze Liver from ze Duck*

It is nine miles of road so flat and treeless that you can see the lights of towns fifteen or twenty miles away on a dark night. I drive it to and from work every day. The people here drive pickups and talk about tractors and horses. A night on the town means a sixty-mile trip to Lubbock to take in some barbecue and a movie. It's who we are and what we do, and I guess I just figured the whole world was that way, too.

A few years back, I was asked to be on an advisory board for a pharmaceutical company. This was, of course, quite an honor, and it meant spending some time in the Northeast. The plane tickets arrived complete with hotel reservations and papers for car rental. They were even footing the bill for my wife to come along.

The hotel was so big that it could sleep the entire town of Lamesa. The company spared no expense: hotel room with two bathrooms, unlimited room service, candy on the pillow, and very impressive dining experiences.

It was the first night there, and we were told that a car would pick us up and take us to our dinner spot. I told Kerri that we might want to dress up a little. She put on a nice pantsuit, and I slipped into a pair of khakis with a pressed Wrangler 20X shirt. A man met us in the hotel lobby and drove us in a limousine about three blocks to a French restaurant.

We were seated with the others on the advisory board, all of whom were wearing suits and ties or evening dresses. "Uncomfortable" was the word that kept coming to mind as they brought us menus and filled our water glasses. The people seated around us were strangers, and none of them looked as though he or she could discuss tractors or horses.

I unfolded the menu, but I couldn't read it. It was in French. I sat there a minute and tried to think if I knew any French words. Hmmmm... nope...not one...not even the cuss words. Kerri made the discovery about the same time I did and started kicking me gently under the table.

Not wanting to appear any more ignorant than I already did in a pair of khakis with white socks, I smiled and pointed to two items on the menu as the waiter graciously jotted something down for our orders.

"What did you get us?" Kerri asked out of the corner of her mouth as the tuxedo-clad waiter made his way around to the rest of our party.

"I have no idea," I muttered under my breath. "Just smile and eat it when it gets here."

About twenty minutes later, the food arrived. Mine was two brown piles of something surrounded by some green leaves. Kerri's was red, and when it arrived, the waiter struck a match to it. It burned brightly for about fifteen seconds before it went out.

As bad as the conversation was, it was pleasant compared to the food. I could barely choke it down. When no one was looking, Kerri slipped her meal into her purse. I paid close attention to how much space she had left in her bag, but I was out of luck; it was full. I continued to eat and disguise my grimace.

When the evening finally ended, I asked the waiter on my way to the door what we had eaten. He smiled and said Kerri had eaten some sort of raw fish. I ate "ze liver from ze duck."

Wow, what are the odds of pointing to two things on a menu and getting two items I would never eat under normal circumstances? It kinda made me wish for nine miles of flat road and a sixty-mile trip to Lubbock, where I can read the menu, wear white socks, and use my wife's purse for nonperishable items.

# Moment 2

*What Can You Do with a Goat in the Kitchen?*

When the doorbell awakens you at 1:00 a.m., it takes a few minutes to get your brain to work.

I first thought it was the alarm and reached over to hit the snooze button. My mind was processing the information and suddenly realized the dinging noise that had corrupted the extreme quiet of the night was not the normal alarm.

I fumbled with my britches as I stumbled down the hall toward the front door. I was pondering that doorbell as I approached the living room half dressed.

"That thing never sounded so loud during the day," passed my lips in a whisper as the obnoxious sound pierced the night once again.

I opened the door, and much to my surprise, a man, a woman, their six children, and a pregnant goat greeted me with wide smiles.

"Our goat is having trouble delivering," the man stated in a concerned tone. "Will you see if you can help her out?"

I ground the sleep out of the corners of my eyes and began to examine ol' "Tiny," the pregnant goat. She fit her name completely. She was a little bitty goat in stature, but large in the belly. She was as big around as she was tall. I went to the pickup and got a palpation sleeve and some lube. I began reaching in to see if these babies were about to be born when Tiny let out a bone-jarring scream. It sounded for all the world like a child screaming. All I could think about was the neighbors. What were the neighbors going to think with a noise like that coming from next door?

It looked like my only option was to invite them in and deliver baby goats in the house. I would have liked to have taken them all to the clinic, but time was of the essence, and I did not think Tiny was going to make it if we didn't do something fast.

Here's the situation: It is one o'clock in the morning, and I am about to deliver baby goats in my living room under the watchful eyes of a family of eight. The children range in age from about twelve all the way down to one.

I had felt enough when palpating Tiny to know that those babies were going to have to come out by cesarean. The garage was out of the question due to countless piles of junk from our recent move. I knew if I got a drop of anything on the carpet, or floor of the kitchen, I would be in big trouble.

I spread newspaper, several layers thick, over the kitchen floor and went to work. There was enough equipment in the vet box of my pickup to do the surgery. I laid Tiny down, clipped and scrubbed the surgical site, gave the proper anesthesia, and then noticed that one of the six children had slipped off into the dining room and was standing on the table.

I decided to ignore the kid and focus on the goat. Every slice with the scalpel brought a chorus of "oohs" from the spectators. They were asking questions about the surgery faster than I could answer. Remember, about ten minutes ago, I was fast asleep, never even suspecting I would be doing a C-section on a goat in the kitchen while a kid danced on the table and his family asked more questions than Alex Trebek on *Jeopardy*.

I finally got the first baby out and handed it off to one of the parents to dry off with the only thing I could find, one of my T-shirts from the laundry room. Drying off the next baby took all the paper towels on the roll hanging under the counter. The last baby was dried off with two dish towels and a pair of socks that had come off that evening with the T-shirt. I used my daughter, Abbi's, little blue nose-sucker thing to get the fluid out of their mouths and throats.

So far, everything was going well. The babies were all alive, and Tiny was doing fine. It was then I noticed that all of the commotion had brought Kerri, my wife, from the bedroom. She was standing at the doorway with one eye on a four-year-old child standing on the table and the other eye on the goo that was flowing across the kitchen floor.

Picture this: the woman of the house, standing in her robe, hair pushed into rugged piles on the left side of her head, puffy eyes from awakening from a deep sleep, trying to imagine why in the world she married a veterinarian.

I felt a lump in my throat as I tried to conjure up a story of how this all had happened. Just as I was about to say something, the family started thanking her repeatedly for letting them use our house to save their goats. Those little children were holding the baby goats with love in their eyes.

There was a faint smell of goat in the house for a couple of weeks. Kerri trashed the T-shirt and socks. I had to mop the kitchen several times to get up the goo. If any neighbors had heard the scream, they never said anything. The footprints on the table came off in time, and Tiny went on to have several more litters of baby goats.

*three*

# Grandparents

# Moment 1

*"Never Put a Pig in Your Mouth," and Other*
*Wise Things Granny Taught You*

The first Thanksgiving after I graduated from vet school brought my two grandmothers, my "city girl" sister, my mother, and my brother for a visit. When you are a new graduate, you get every weekend and holiday on call because everyone else is tired of not being home enough.

My grandmothers were just "so proud" of their grandson, a recent veterinary school graduate. No one in my family had ever finished college, much less gone for eight years. They thought I could do no wrong and wanted to go with me on every call.

As is always the case when you have special plans for Thanksgiving Day, the phone rang at 8:00 p.m. It was a woman from a town about forty-five minutes away with a gilt pig that was not having luck delivering. She informed me that this was no ordinary litter. The daddy of these babies was the greatest of all pigs, and he had died since this batch was conceived. If we didn't get a little boy pig, his genes would be gone—forever. No pressure.

Of course, my entire family wanted to go observe the pig situation. One grandmother was about five feet tall and weighed about 180 pounds, while the other one was about six feet tall and weighed about one hundred pounds. Boy, did they make a pair!

We met the pig's family at the clinic. The woman was wearing an EMT outfit. (This turned out to be a vital indicator of the future events of the evening.) She was a tall, big woman with a gruff voice. Her EMT garb included a stethoscope and a pocket protector with all sorts of medical equipment. She was all business. My grandmothers were right in there helping and assisting.

I reached into the pig and realized that there was no way those piglets were coming out that way. I told the EMT woman that we were going to have to do a C-section. She got even more serious and reminded me that her world-famous boar hog had died. No pressure.

My grandmothers were both in the background saying, "He can do it. He's the best doctor in the world." Eeeeeh, no pressure.

I prepared the gilt and cut her open. Once inside, I could tell that there were only three babies, and I conveyed that information.

"Well, one of 'em better be a live boy," the EMT woman said.

No pressure.

I cut open the uterus and pulled out a dead girl. The next piglet was another little girl, and she was not doing very well. One pig left. One chance at a boy. The tension mounted as I struggled to get the last pig out. Finally, it arrived. Much to my relief, it was a boy. But he was not doing well, either.

Suddenly, this large EMT woman came swooping across the room and grabbed the piglet from my shaking hands. She rushed it over to the counter and began giving chest compressions. The pair of grandmothers watched intently.

She counted, "a one, and a two, and a three," as she gave these chest compressions with her first two fingers. The pair of grandmothers was still very intent. Then, as if in a CPR instructional video, she picked up the piglet, stuck his entire head in her mouth, and began blowing.

This was more than the outspoken grandmothers could stand. They made that grandmother noise. It's kinda a cross between Tarzan and a high-pitched yodel. You've heard it. It was the noise they made when you were a kid and did something gross like pick your nose or spit ice back into your Coke.

The next few moments happened in slow motion for me.

My "city girl" sister was retching over the sink while holding her hair back so not to get anything on it. My mother was saying, "Oh my goodness," over and over. My brother was laughing, but my grandmothers were aghast.

The EMT woman slapped the piglet back onto the counter and began chest compressions again. My grandmothers performed as a team. One wiped afterbirth off the woman's cheek, while the other said, "You shouldn't put a pig in your mouth!"

Just as they were about to get her clean, she picked the piglet back up and put him in her mouth again. This brought another harmonious grandma Tarzan call.

I could hear them saying, together this time, "Oh, honey, you just shouldn't put a pig in your mouth!" They offered to go to the store and get her a toothbrush.

The pig lived. The EMT woman was happy. But my grandmothers would never be the same.

# Moment 2

*Nonny*

Our upbringing shapes the way we see life and react to it. The people responsible for raising us leave an indelible mark on our beings. My grandmother, Nonny, grew up in a family of five sisters and one brother. These people helped shape me and gave me my perspective on life. They were rural, moral, salt-of-the-earth people who held firm to their beliefs and spent their entire lifetimes honing their keen senses of humor.

This moment in time starts with the lone brother, J. W., making a trip to the booming city of Amarillo, Texas, to stay with two of the sisters while his wife underwent some testing at a hospital there. One of the sisters was Nonny and the other, Jo Anna. For as long as I can remember, they were naggers. Not mean or ugly, just a little hardheaded, and if something wasn't just like they thought it should be, they would tell you about it over and over until you fixed it like they wanted.

Every time I would see them, they would go on and on about my moustache, or my constant wearing of a cap, or me working too many hours. They would do it until it almost drove me crazy. If they didn't like something, they would harp on it endlessly.

J. W. was a farmer/rancher and didn't come to town very often. He was about to leave to go to the hospital, when they noticed the tools in his pickup. Things like a saddle, some wrenches, a few bits, some plow shanks, maybe a saw or two were just sitting in the back of the truck and in the cab. When they saw this, the nagging started.

"J. W., you better lock that stuff up before you go to the hospital, or someone will steal it. You ain't in Brice, Texas. This is the big city, and people are just aching to take stuff like that."

This went on and on as he drove out of the driveway. I am sure after growing up with this bunch, he had learned to let it go in one ear and out the other.

The sisters left a little while later and found J. W.'s pickup in the parking lot of the hospital. They parked next to it and checked the doors. Sure enough, he hadn't locked them. And there in the back was all that stuff just waiting to be pilfered. Being the crafty women they were, they decided to just take all those tools out and put them in their trunk. Yeah, that would show him not to leave all that stuff unattended in the big city.

I wish I could have seen those two old women packing all that stuff out of that truck into their trunk. It must have taken them thirty minutes. Some of that stuff was heavy, but they managed to take every bit of it.

Next, it was up to the room with sly smirks on their faces and a wait until he went down to leave. They would giggle for no reason at times, just waiting for him to learn his lesson about "locking them things up."

About an hour later, one of the sisters looked out the window of the room, which overlooked the parking lot, and noticed that J. W.'s pickup was gone.

"Why, J. W., someone stole your pickup," came rolling out of Nonny's mouth as she gazed at the empty spot next to her car.

He strolled to the window and said, "No, they didn't. I parked over there, next to the fence."

There were only two people in that hospital room who felt the impact of J. W.'s statement. Their faces went white, and they looked like two little girls who were about to be sent to the principal's office. Their trunk now held all the tools from some other country bumpkin's pickup—and he was gone. How would they ever find him to give all that stuff back? Worse yet, what if he came back with the police and they found all of that stuff in *their* car?

I laugh hard every time I think about that moment. They actually called the TV station and asked them to put the event on the six o'clock news so that whomever they had robbed could get his stuff back. The TV station obviously declined, so they had to call the police, explain the entire humiliating event, and hand the stuff over.

Nonny died on the last day of 2005. She was over ninety and still just as feisty as the day she robbed some cowboy of all his tools. We miss her deeply.

# Moment 3

*Mamaw*

My mamaw used to iron Papaw's work clothes for him every day. He was a farmer/rancher! We left early in the morning to go work and didn't get home until after dark. Most days, Papaw never saw anyone but me and maybe a few other crusty farmers. I could never understand why she needed to iron

She used starch that she mixed up and put in a glass Coke bottle with this cork/metal headmetal cap that slipped into the mouth of the bottle and had a multitude of holes in it, like a saltshaker. She would sprinkle his pants with the starch and hang them over a chair for a few minutes so they could dry a bit before she applied the heat of the iron to them.

I would watch her do this when I was a little kid and considered it normal. I just figured that every old woman in the world did it because this was all I had ever known. As the years passed, I began to question this practice. Why in the world did work clothes need to be ironed? Mamaw never ironed mine, and there was no way I saw any use to doing this myself. Heck, my clothes were usually so dirty by 9:00 a.m. that any sign of ironing would be long gone.

One day when I was about thirteen years old, I asked her about it. I wanted to know why she thought it necessary to invest time and effort pressing clothes that would never be seen and would be filthy in just a short time.

Her reply was as sweet a sentiment as I have found. She told me that Papaw was the most handsome man in the world. She said he was her best friend and the love of her life. She loved every chance she got to show him off and make the rest of the world jealous because he was hers. She went on to say that you just never knew when, at some point in the day, he was gonna run into people, and she wanted him to look the part of the most handsome man God ever made.

I looked closely at him later that day. He sure didn't look all that handsome to me. He was a short, skinny man with a relatively big fanny compared to his shoulders. His hair was thin on top, and his false teeth didn't line up too good when he smiled. He wore horn-rimmed glasses that were much too big for his face because all he really cared about was being able to see. I really didn't see how anyone could consider this man the most handsome one God ever made.

I asked her about it a few days later. I informed her that I had closely observed ol' Elmo Brown and most certainly didn't see him as the most handsome man on Earth.

She giggled and gave me a girlish smile that grandmothers just shouldn't be able to express at that age.

"You just aren't looking in the right light, Turdhead. He is the most beautiful man God ever made. Those eye wrinkles haven't always been there. I remember when he had real teeth. He has the most beautiful blue eyes I have ever seen. They are exactly the same color as the sky just before the sun goes down. His entire face lights up when he smiles, and his voice is so calming and full that everyone in nine counties wants to hear him talk."

What? He was my papaw. He had always been an old man as far as I was concerned. I never knew him any other way. Was she actually wanting me to consider that Papaw used to be young? Ha ha ha ha, no way.

"I want him to feel beautiful! I iron his clothes every day because for all these years, he has made me feel that way, beautiful. He is a man worthy of respect. I want him to look the part every day. I wouldn't have it any other way."

Meant nothing to me. I heard it and was kinda grossed out a bit. This was ridiculous to me, and I just decided to forget I had ever asked. How could this old woman think that an old man with false teeth was beautiful? Sheesh...old people.

I watched them grow old together and die. I was probably thirty when it dawned on me what beauty really was. And it was her ironing his pants with starch from a Coke bottle that taught me how to see the world that way.

# Moment 4

*Papaw*

"Good throw!" Papaw shouted as I completed my first back-of-the-pickup rope sling.

On the first attempt, I caught the sick calf around the neck. I was about twelve years old, and no words could have made my head swell bigger than any kind of "atta boy" from him.

I called him Papaw, and he called me "Turdhead." He was my hero. He had the patience of Job as he taught me how to work. He taught me to whirl that rope and size my loop. He taught me to keep my slack until just the right moment when I should close it down on my target.

It has been a while since he died. Just today, I remembered him deeply with the fond memories that can come only after the sting of loss has passed, revealing the voice he left to guide me. It was this little voice I heard with each item I removed from the trailer.

My wife, Kerri, and I finally got a storage house. The day after he died, I loaded up all the things out of the barn that he had told me would be mine when he passed on. They were all packed neatly into a stock trailer that had belonged to his dad. The trailer and all my treasures had been in storage since a few days after he died.

It took me hours to move those pieces of our history from the trailer to the storage house. Each nugget brought back a moment that he and I had spent together, Papaw teaching me, and me not even knowing there was a lesson in progress. He made learning the lessons of life such fun that it was years later, after I had grown into a man, that I realized how much he had taught me and how much time he spent doing it.

As I dug through the pile, I uncovered a bottle of "Thermic Liniment." It must have been thirty years old. He used it on every sore horse we ever had; said it "pulled out the swellin'."

He could fix anything that was ailing. He was particular about how to care for our animals. Everything had to be done correctly and at the right time. Even though he had no idea, Papaw was instilling in me a lifetime mission of seeing to the needs of animals. He gave me an incredible interest in caring for critters that lives on today.

He had an incredible way of seeing the world. I would hear him describe an event, and his description was much better than actually living through the moment had been. I used to love to hear him tell someone else about an event that he and I had lived through together. Listening to him made me aware that I was not watching the world closely enough.

He would often ask me what I thought the horse I was on might be thinking. He would tell me that if I would look at things through the horse's eyes, it would open up an entirely new world. Through the eyes of critters, I would find an entirely new perspective.

"Good throw!" Papaw shouted as I completed my first back-of-the-pickup rope sling around the sick calf's neck. The thing he had not told me was what to do next. The calf may have been sick, but he still weighed five hundred pounds, and I weighed in at about eighty-five. I watched as the coils of rope in my hand got smaller and smaller and the calf got farther and farther away. In a panic, I dallied to the nearest thing in sight, a CB antenna coming off the headache rack. Well, it wasn't a whole antenna, just the spring that made up the base. The antenna had broken off years before. This, of course, didn't even slow the calf down. As the tension hit the antenna, the knot on the end of the rope hit my hand. Not wanting to disappoint my hero, I held on to that knot for dear life.

The next thing I remember was a moment of peaceful flying. The CB antenna, the bracket that held it on, and the driver's-side mirror that was hung up on my boot hit the ground like Johnny Bench sliding into home plate. All I could hear was, "Let go of the rope, Turdhead!" He was saying it over and over, and the sound was getting softer and softer as the calf pulled me in the direction of his momma. By now, letting go was not an option. The bracket of the antenna had wedged between my hand and the rope, and I was being pulled along like a rag doll.

The only thing I remember hurting while I was being pulled was my left ear. Somehow, in the fall it had filled up with dirt and grass. I must have been surfing on that ear for about a hundred yards before any other part of my body hit the ground. The dragging began to slow as the calf wore down. He finally stopped well short of his momma.

Being twelve years old and made of rubber, I hopped right up and jumped on him like a rodeo clown. By the time Pawpaw got there, I had the calf tied up and was working him over. If you can tell how bad a dragging is by the amount of dirt in your underwear, this one was monumental. I had enough in my britches to grow potatoes! It was filling up my boots as I got up to walk away.

I miss him. I miss his view of life. I miss being called Turdhead. I wish I had told him how much he influenced me and how I watched him and hung on his every word. He got to see me become a veterinarian.

In his own way, he displayed how proud he was without ever saying those words. I wish he were here now to read the words he spoke as we rode through the weeds and mosquitoes and see how they have given me a whole new perspective. I wish he were here now to give me guidance and fill my world with his thoughts, but I guess I'll have to settle for the voice he left to guide me.

# Moment 5

*More Papaw*

There are just some things that make a difference, things you will never forget. Maybe they are things that when they occur, a person doesn't realize how amazing they are. This moment was one of those.

I was about three-quarters of the way through my first year of vet school. It had been hard. My dad had died the previous year, and all the money my mother had for the rest of her life was a measly life insurance policy.

I had worked hard to have enough money to make it through that first year of vet school. I knew I couldn't get much financial help because that life insurance policy made it look like my mother had made a huge amount of money in one year, and it made me unqualified for grants or loans. I was broke. And I mean broke.

I was eating oatmeal and riding a frickin' moped to school. I had saved enough money working through high school and undergraduate school that I thought I could make that first year, but I was running out of money in March, and my stress level was high.

It was a Monday night and my papaw called me. This was a big event for everyone because he hated talking on the phone. We small-talked for a few minutes, and then he suddenly asked me how much money I needed. What? How could this old man know that I was in a money crunch? I had not told a soul of my moped riding and oatmeal eating.

I told him that things were pretty tough. I told him that I wasn't gonna ask my momma for money because she needed what she had for the rest of her life. What he said next just hit me in the heart. I was so tired. I had been studying hard for days and trying to deal with being totally without money. I was wondering if this would ever pay off and how I was gonna make three more years of it.

He told me not to worry. He said he would have some money to me by Friday and that I should eat some beef or something that was not just oatmeal. He laughed about the moped and told me to get my truck fixed with the money he was sending. He had a way. His way was calming and secure.

On Friday, the check arrived. I figured I needed about $1,000 to make it through, and then I could get a job for the summer. I opened the envelope. In it was a check for $10,000. *Ten thousand dollars.* It was the largest single check I had ever seen, and it was made out to me.

I had worked with this man all of my life. He had paid me like a hired hand, and I had always had everything I needed. I never asked for money, and he never offered it. I had worked my way through college and bought my truck and horses. I was holding a check in my hand that said more than money. It said more than grandson. It said, "Bo, I believe in you. You are gonna make it, and I am proud of you."

I finished that semester with a 4.0 grade point average. I sent him my report card and told him he was my hero.

I will never forget the load that left my shoulders when that check from an old cowboy from West Texas lifted my spirits. That moment gave me a strength that I will never forget. It was an amazing moment.

My mamaw told me later that he put my report card from vet school in his ranch truck. She said he showed it to everyone in the county anytime he had the chance. She said she had never seen Elmo Brown brag about anything in her life, but he bragged about his grandson every day. Wow! That was worth more than $10,000 to me.

*four*

Kids

# Moment 1

### They Do Listen to Songs

We have three daughters (ages eight, eleven, and thirteen), and I am always amazed at what goes through the minds of children. They see things in their world and store those thoughts to be brought up at the strangest times. We had an episode a few weeks ago that made me reevaluate what kids are really thinking.

A few Fridays ago, the phone rang at about 11:00 p.m. It was Dr. Marty Ivey from Ruidoso, New Mexico, with a horse suffering from colic that appeared to need surgery. Translation: The critter would get to Lamesa around 3:00 a.m. I told him to send it on, and we would be glad to try to make that horse happy again.

The carrier arrived at the expected time and unloaded a very sick racehorse. We got the horse in the stocks, and sure enough, the exam revealed a twisted gut. This is not a good thing if you are a horse. Surgery is about the only option, and sometimes it offers little hope.

After an extensive examination, I told the horse carrier that surgery was going to be the only option.

"This is a very special horse," the road-weary man muttered. "I sure hope you can fix it."

Every horse is a really special horse in the eyes of someone. I understand it, and when I hear it, I move on.

"This horse belongs to Toby Keith." The carrier slurred the words from exhaustion, but the message was sharp enough. I started feeling pressure.

I could just visualize a video starring me, with a stupid look on my face, plastered all over Country Music Television. Mr. Keith tells the interviewer: "Yeah, that's him. He's that vet from Lamesa, Texas, who killed my prize racehorse." Worse yet, I might become the brunt of some country song that Willie Nelson and Toby write about "the redneck vet from West Texas." What if it became a hit and lived on for generations?

The crew gathered, and we did the surgery, just as we have on hundreds of other horses. The surgery went well, and I was feeling fairly optimistic about the horse's condition when we left that Saturday evening.

When I arrived home, I gathered the three Brock girls together to tell them the news. You see, they love Toby Keith and have all his CDs. I just knew they would have a few "wows" for the story.

Much to my surprise, this is not what I got from my eight-year-old, Kimmi.

"I knew that was going to happen," she said in a matter-of-fact tone. It almost sounded like she had been expecting it for some time.

What in the world would elicit this reaction from an eight-year-old? How could she ever even suppose that Toby Keith's horse would wind up in Lamesa? She had heard about many colic surgeries but never one on a celebrity's horse. My wife, Kerri, and I sat there for a moment with wondering looks on our faces, when Kimmi broke the silence with her reasoning.

"Yeah, I knew that was going to happen; you're not supposed to give beer to horses."

For those of you who have not heard the song, it goes: "Whiskey for my men; beer for my horses." I have never been sure what it means, but Kimmi heard it and figured it was just a matter of time before that horse developed gut problems and would be headed to Lamesa to see her daddy.

The older sisters, Emili and Abbi, immediately chimed in. "He didn't really give beer to his horse; that is just a song."

"No, it's not. Why would he say it if he didn't do it?" Kimmi fired back.

The puzzled looks on our faces were replaced with wide-mouthed, eye-squinting laughter.

There you have it: the mind of a child. I love it.

The horse did well and went back home to Toby. We never actually heard from him, but as far as Kimmi was concerned, I should have called him and informed him that whiskey for the men might be OK, but he'd better stay away from giving beer to the horses.

# Moment 2

*Stinky Dad*

**D**o you remember the things during childhood that made your father special? Perhaps it was the sound of his voice whispering good night, the way his footsteps sounded across the floor as he approached your room, or the look on his face that meant you'd better straighten up.

Or perhaps it was his smell—the way he smelled in the morning when he hugged you before leaving for work. Usually it was just his shaving cream, cologne, or deodorant, but it was a fresh scent, and it was Dad. Depending on what your father did for a living, it might be in sharp contrast to the smell he came home with at night.

I hadn't realized how conditioned our children had become to the rituals of life until the other evening when I returned from work to find a houseful of little girls. My own girls were having some friends over for a slumber party. There they were, eleven girls between the ages of four and nine, all talking continuously.

All of the details were well planned. I started to work right away on the tent that we were to pitch atop the trampoline. Can you think of anything cooler than sleeping in a tent on a trampoline? Five or six of the girls came over to help me set it up.

Our oldest, Emili, was next to me, helping hold the things needed for assembly. She hugged me and told me she was glad I was her dad. Soon, another girl was close to me, holding a rope. I noticed she had a huge frown on her face and was holding her nose.

When I asked what was wrong, she said, "You stink, bad."

Funny, Emili just hugged me and hadn't mentioned a thing. I just figured the other kid was a soft-nose and went on with the tent assembly. But a minute later, another kid was close by, and I noticed the same look.

"What's wrong with you?" I asked.

"I don't mean to be rude, Mr. Brock, but you smell worse than anything in the world," she said.

I decided it was time for a little research. I walked over to our middle child and gave her a "pick up and swing you" hug. She just smiled and hugged me back. Not a word about my aroma.

Next, I went over to Kimmi, our youngest, and did the same. Again, not a mention of any BO (no pun intended).

Some of the other girls thought the spinning hug looked like fun and wanted to take a turn, but when they came down from the spin, most said something about how bad Abbi's dad smelled.

Admittedly, it had been a stinky day. Pigs, postmortems, cow palpations, abscesses, and who-knows-what-else had been on the agenda that day. Picking up the pungent odors one at a time, my nose didn't seem to register them. I'm sure all were bound together by a layer of perspiration after a near-one-hundred-degree day.

It made me stop and reflect on my girls' lack of reaction. They probably think that every father should come home smelling like a carcass. It probably even comforts them—here comes Daddy home from work, and, if everything is OK, he will smell like manure.

I began to think about other conditions they consider normal that others might not: They can eat a hamburger while watching a calf being born. They can pick up blood-soaked gauze while helping clean up and never bat an eye. They have seen more shots given than most people who are fifty years old. They have helped me do C-sections on cows.

There will be a time that such a stinky dad will be a huge embarrassment to them, I am sure. But when that phase passes, and they are grown-ups with kids of their own, I am sure they will come back to finding some strange degree of comfort in the smells that an animal hospital fills their noses with.

# Moment 3

*Fishing*

It was a Saturday afternoon, and I was gonna take Emili and Abbi (the oldest two daughters) fishing. In West Texas, that is a really huge undertaking because there are no fishing holes very close. A family in Seminole had opened a fishing pond, and it sounded like the kind of fun I wanted the girls to encounter.

Kerri was gone with the youngest girl, and I had rounded up all the fishing equipment and was ready to see how many catfish we could haul in at the newly opened fishing hole. I spent days telling them about it and showing them how to cast and bring in the line. I told them that if we caught any, we were gonna fry them up and have them for supper. I told them I couldn't wait to show them how to clean and cook a catfish.

We were all anticipating the adventure. As a solo practitioner in small-town America, I should have known better than to look forward to anything. Just as we loaded the last fishing pole in the truck, the phone rang. A cow C-section was on the way. How do you explain to two little souls that the fishing trip is off, and we have to go work on a cow?

As usual, they were both understanding. They had never known anything different. Daddy was always having to leave and go work on som'in' sick. They had just come to expect it. But it really irked me! I was totally excited about taking them fishing.

I explained to them that we were gonna do a surgery on this cow, and as soon as we were done, we would head to the fishing hole. I decided that if we couldn't fish now, we would later, and I would let them suture the incision on the cow.

The cow arrived exactly an hour later than the grumpy ol' rancher said it would. He unloaded her and hollered at me that he was going home; he had plans with his family. Man, that just made things even better.

The girls and I loaded the angry cow into the chute. She wanted no part of humans and was gonna whoop anything that got in her way. I don't really blame her. We finally got her captured, and she promptly lay down. If you haven't done much vet work on a cow, you probably don't know that when a cow lies down in the squeeze chute, you are in a mess. There is no way to do a C-section on a cow lying down in a squeeze chute. She either has to stand up, or be rope tied and lying on her right side so the incision can be made in her left flank.

This cow would not cooperate at all. So, I explained to the girls how to tie her feet and restrain her so we could help her. I went about getting the ropes around her feet and legs, and then we gradually opened the side gate to the squeeze chute. The cow finally decided that she couldn't do it alone and somehow determined that we were there to help her.

We had her calmed down and restrained. I began to explain why the calf wouldn't come out. I let them both put a palpation sleeve–covered arm into her birth canal before we laid her down so they could see how twisted up the calf was and that it was much too big to come out that way.

I am not sure they understood then, but when they have kids someday, they will surely remember this poor cow. They were both completely focused on getting that calf out of there. It was amazing to me how five- and seven-year-old children were so in tune to birth and the introduction of a new life into this world.

I really felt a meaning to this moment with them. I felt like they were young, but ready to be introduced to the world of babies being born. I spent a few minutes realizing how everything like this was new to them. It was a thought-provoking realization that they were going to remember this day with me for life.

When I was in the third grade, a boy in my class was sent to the principal for saying the *F* word. I went home and asked my momma what it meant. She told me that the two dogs that were stuck together on the back porch a few months ago were doing that, and that it was how animals made babies.

I grew up thinking that someday I was gonna get stuck together with a woman that way in order to make a baby. It made me really aware of what my girls would take away from this event.

I went over how we were gonna get the baby out. I went over how it got in there in the first place. I described the difference in skin thickness between cows and people. I told them about a uterus and an ovary. I told them how sperm coupled with an egg. I did all this without ever saying any of those grown-up words while we were actually getting that calf out of the predicament it was in. They never even knew I was teaching them a thing.

I let them make the incision though the skin. I told them how lidocaine killed pain. I talked about how muscles made an animal move. I showed them the stomach after we got in and told them how that was where food went when they swallowed. I taught them about sterility after we shaved her hair and scrubbed her side with iodine. We cut open her uterus, and I watched their faces as we pulled a living calf out of a cow and assisted God in bringing a life into this world. I told them how the baby was surrounded by fluid and getting blood from the momma through the belly button so it didn't need air until it was out on its own and breathing.

I hung that calf upside down so the fluid could run out of its lungs and had them hold it there and suck the juice out of its nose and mouth so it could breathe. These two kids were completely dissolved in the moment of birth. They were building a memory that would influence their essences and color their imaginations for always.

We finished, and everything went well. We were cleaning up and washing away all the stuff that comes out when a baby is born. I noticed that Emili, the oldest, had left a spot of blood on her left, white tennis shoe. I asked her why she didn't clean that off.

She replied, "I am gonna show that to everyone at school on Monday. There are lots of kids that can go fishing with their dads, but I am the only kid around that got to deliver a baby calf with my daddy this weekend."

I thought about that statement a lot. So many veterinarians say that their careers kept them from having any time with the family. They gripe and complain because they can't go fishing often enough or take vacations. And I agree. It is overwhelming. But, oh my, how they have missed the opportunity to let those children take part in some of the most wonderful moments that life has to offer. Remember, anyone can go fishing on a Saturday afternoon. But how many kids get to help Daddy bring a new critter into this world and watch it take its very first breath?

# Moment 4

## *What Kind of Heinie?*

**B**ecause my daughters were growing up with a mixed-animal veterinarian for a father, I thought they had seen just about every anatomical part of a mammal. I was wrong; there was one that our youngest girl, Kimmi, had not yet seen.

With two sisters, a mother, and six girl cousins, Kimmi had never been exposed to human "boy parts." Finally, we had a boy cousin. Kimmi was four years old when the little tyke came to the house to spend a few days.

She was sitting in the big chair watching television and eating Cheetos when my wife plopped the new baby boy on the floor to change a wet diaper. I looked across the room just in time to see Kimmi's focus go from cartoons to the now-half-naked baby. With her head cocked to one side like a dog hearing a high-pitched sound, she developed a curious expression as the Cheetos consumption came to a gradual stop.

I could feel a smile sliding in on one side of my mouth and could hardly wait to see what she would do next. She slid off the chair, licking one hand clean of Cheetos residue and the other grasping the half-empty bag. She made her way over and bent at the waist to get a closer look.

It is always funny to me to watch a little kid process new information. This was not the normal anatomy, and she knew it. She just couldn't decide what had happened to cause it. She just stood there, still licking orange off her hand, and watched as Kerri cleaned and readied the area for a new diaper. Several times it looked as if she was about to say something, but the thought never gathered enough organization to form a sentence.

Finally, after several minutes, she cut her eyes to Kerri and said, "What kind of heinie is *that*?"

Not wanting to miss an opportunity to be a father, I filled in the answer. "That's an evil heinie...You stay away from heinies like that."

She looked at me with a puzzled, almost terrified look. She walked away from it almost as if it would jump off and attack her. Kerri went on to explain what kind of heinie it really was. We laughed about it for days, but it made me think a bit about having three daughters and what an adventure it is going to be when boys come courting.

The more I thought about it, the more it worried me. Here they were, *my* three beautiful girls, and someday, *boys* were going to want to date them. What was I going to do? So I composed a sign and put it over the front door:

**CAUTION:**
**I'VE CASTRATED THOUSANDS**
**OF ANIMALS.**
**IF YOU WANT TO DATE MY DAUGHTER,**
**DON'T BE AN**
**ANIMAL.**

# Moment 5

*Brandon and the Fly*

My brother is ten years younger than I am, and his brain could eat my brain and not be full. He has more letters after his name than anyone I know. He is a professor at some institute of neurology and can say more big words in one sentence than anyone I have ever met. I was watching him be interviewed on a *Good Morning America*-type show the other day about the death of some celebrity and was amazed at how many adjectives came out of his mouth before he finally got to the noun they described.

As I watched this interview with "Dr. Brandon Brock," my mind drifted back to watching him grow up and turn into this famous doctor who fixes people with broken brains. We are much different. I live in a tiny town in West Texas and try to avoid crowds of people at all costs; he lives in Dallas, Texas, and flies all over the world giving lectures on neurology.

As I watched him settin' there all dressed up and on TV, I remembered all the times he would come to Lamesa and hang out with me at the clinic when he was a kid. When I moved to Lamesa, he was still in high school, and he would spend days or weeks at a time working with me and getting a taste of rural America.

On the day this particular story occurred (about 1992), you would have never convinced me that he would someday grow up to be so smart. We were out at an ostrich farm, of all places. These people raised ostriches back in the days that they were worth $20,000 apiece. They had giant incubators and barns built with heated floors and central air. They were having some trouble with a few of the chicks getting crippled and had called me out to have a look. I took Brandon with me because I knew we were gonna have to do some running to catch these things, and he was a fast rascal.

The baby ostriches were in pens about thirty feet long and maybe fifteen feet wide. There were little fences about three feet high between the pens, and each pen had about ten ostriches in it. You have to remember that the owner of these ostriches was a detail man. He wanted everything just right and kept things so neat and clean that you could eat off the floor.

The owner gave an extensive history of the problem and then said we needed to catch one of the crippled birds and examine it. I sent Brandon into the pen and told him to catch it and bring it over to us so we could have a look.

Well, Brandon immediately went into overdrive. He hopped over the short fence with nothing on his mind but catching the ostrich we had identified. He was so focused that he didn't see the supersticky fly tape thing that was hanging down over the pen. In fact, he didn't see the next supersticky fly thing or the next one after that.

He managed to run into the first one with the top of his head. Those things are so sticky that, once they get in your hair, they will stay with you no matter what. The next one caught him on the front of his shirt, and the third one across his forehead.

It was the impact and adherence of that third one that brought him to a standstill. He reached up to attempt to pull the amazingly sticky thing from his forehead, never considering that it would also stick to his hand when he touched it. As he tried to pull it off, it just slid down until it was over his eyes and sticking to his eyebrows and eyelashes. He then took his other hand to attempt to release the one stuck to the top of his head.

This was the situation: His right hand was stuck to the fly tape that was also stuck to his eyes. His left hand was stuck to the fly tape that was also stuck to his hair. Attempts to pull on either one resulted in hair-pulling pain and no apparent way to escape. Not only that, but he could no longer see, so he ran into the wall and became stuck to it by the third one that was bound to his shirt and neck.

He was hollering for help, but he wasn't gonna get it from me for a while, because I was laughing so hard I couldn't do anything. The fella who owned the place was no help, either; he was laughing just as hard as I was. We just stood there for a few minutes laughing and seeing what he was gonna do next.

I wasn't going to touch him because sticky stuff like that grosses me out. The owner dude must have felt the same because he just kinda stood there, too. Brandon was pleading with us to get the fly tape off him gently, but neither of us was able to do anything but laugh.

Finally, we got some rags and managed to pull them all loose from his body. He hollered for us to slow down while we pulled one off with clumps of hair and eyebrows still attached to it, but we assured him that ripping it off with one fast motion would be less painful.

We finally finished and headed home. Brandon could barely open his eyes because the residual sticky stuff had his eyelashes matted together. And look at him now, I thought. He was on TV, saying more big words than anyone I have ever known.

# *Section 3*

## Animals

You can always tell a pioneer by the arrows in his ass.

Chuck Deyhle
1990

*five*

## Horses

# Moment 1

*Through the Eyes of a Horse*

The woman told me that it must be tough to work on critters, since they can't tell you what is wrong. She went on to say, "Don't you wish they could just talk and tell you what is bothering them?"

I had pondered this many times, so my answer was certainly not spontaneous. The answer was brief: "*No.*"

My grandmother was sick in Amarillo, Texas, and I was visiting her in the hospital there. I sat in a chair at the foot of her bed for quite a long time, and she had long since dozed off. I listened to the hospital, listened to the people who were occupants of those beds. I spent a long time absorbing their requests, complaints, dislikes, aggravations, hunger pains, bathroom requests, hot and cold needs, and just endless ramblings.

One woman went on a fifteen-minute tirade over the temperature of her apple juice; she went on and on about how no one could possibly drink apple juice at room temperature. An older fella was constantly griping about the texture of the sheets on his bed—they were too crisp and brittle (whatever those adjectives mean when describing bedding). A middle-aged man whined about the TV, and how it didn't get ESPN. He grumbled and pined and tried to strike a deal with the nurse to get a computer with an Internet connection so he could watch a football game.

An elderly woman was walking down the hall pushing an IV stand beside her and complaining about the excessive degree of friction the wheels on the stand had on the carpet. Several rooms down, a child cried and screamed because the nurse wanted him to swallow a pill.

The man in the room with my grandmother was griping all evening about how hot it was, while my grandmother was freezing to death.

I listened to a fifteen-minute conversation between nurses outside the door of our room about a woman in an adjacent room who wanted to talk to a doctor because she was afraid that the incision from a surgery was gonna leave a scar.

I sat in that chair and pondered what it would be like if horses could talk. Can you even imagine? Oh, my goodness, what would they say at our clinic?

"Hey, Doc, thanks for getting that chip outta my knee, but could you do som'in' about that horse in the stall next to me? That rascal has been pacing all night, and it is driving me nuts."

"Dr. Brock, I want to register a complaint about the alfalfa. It is way too stemmy, and there's a little twang of Johnson grass wafting in the aftertaste."

"Hey, Bo, I am totally against an orange bandage. I cannot believe I am paying good money for a bandage, and you guys make it stand out like a road cone."

"Doc, could you do som'in' about the radio station? We been listening to country music here for three days, and all I am asking is a single day of soft rock!"

"Is there any way someone could please take me for a walk in the front of the hospital? I love watching the cars go by, and you can't see the road from the back pasture!"

It didn't take me long to answer that woman's question about wishing critters could talk. I will gladly put up with having to unravel the mystery of where things hurt because it means not listening to all of the complaints about meaningless fodder that would come with speech.

# Moment 2

*Randy*
*A eulogy by Emily Berryhill, an intern at Brock Veterinary Clinic*

Just this past Sunday, the clinic horse, Randy, passed away on his own without fuss, next to his pile of alfalfa, and with his good friend, Elvis, the donkey, standing by. To clinic visitors, he was probably just another older horse standing in the back pasture, a sorrel-and-white paint with an occasional limp to his right front leg. If you went down to the pasture and looked closely, however, you would see that Randy had a lightning-bolt freeze brand on his cheek, that he was lame in the right front due to a knobby knee, that his blue eyes were sensitive to the sun and the dust, and that his feet grew into pancakes when they got too long. If you had the time and inclination to spend time with him, you would notice that he ate his alfalfa much more voraciously than the grass hay, actually halfway listened to the stall cleaner when he spoke, and depended on his little buddy, Elvis, for security and fun.

Randy was an integral part of Brock Veterinary Clinic for fifteen years or so, after being surrendered due to a severe hoof injury. This eulogy to him stemmed from a single sentence Bo spoke: "He taught me to rope."

In fact, Randy was responsible for the teaching of many. His initial role as instructor did, indeed, come in the form of roping. From what I'm told, he and Bo were staples at the rodeo arena, catching steers and dallying ropes almost nightly for several years. Randy taught Bo to head. He also taught him what a broken tailbone felt like. They were partners, a man and his horse, both in it for the thrill of the moment.

As time passed, Randy's role transitioned. He became the go-to horse when the clinic got new equipment that needed to be tried out.

He was an instructional tool for clinic staff and veterinarians. That right knee likely had as many radiographs taken of it for testing purposes as all the racehorses that came through in a year's time. Tendons were ultrasounded as machines were compared, and Randy once had full-body infrared laser therapy as a woman peddled her wares.

Randy continued to serve the role of teacher to visiting students eager to put their hands on a horse and be a real veterinarians. His saucer feet were slowly nipped and rasped; his front limbs often abducted significantly more than seemed comfortable. Vaccinations were popped into his neck, sometimes vigorously and other times tentatively. His teeth were floated in fits and starts as students learned to manipulate the power tools, and he always stayed sedated like a champion, rather than bouncing around as soon as the speculum was opened.

Finally, Randy was instrumental in teaching me how to relax and let a day go by. Our evening routine, be it in summer, when the air was still hot at 10:00 p.m., or in winter, when fingers were too cold to buckle blankets, involved a large senior mash for him, Elvis scavenging whatever fell out of Randy's mouth, and me chasing off the occasional extra horse in the pasture to ensure that Randy got his meal. Those quiet times when the stars and moon shone bright, as they can do only in Texas, and all that's heard are the soft noises of a horse munching his feed, brought about a peace that I can still feel. When I was at my limit from a string of busy nights with little sleep or I'd had a particularly frustrating day, as everyone occasionally does, Randy's shoulder absorbed hot tears, and his dusty coat and pure horse scent again brought comfort.

In the eyes of many, Randy was just a horse. But to Brock Veterinary Clinic, he was anything but that. He lived a good life, and had an easy death, which is in itself a blessing. He is now buried in his pasture, with his buddy Elvis standing by, and will be thought of daily by the man who tossed him his breakfast, the intern who cared for him most recently, the other vets as their eyes scan the horses around them, by Bo as he leans against the pasture fence talking on the phone, and by me, three states away, when I see a paint horse with a blue eye. And his imaginary tombstone reads forever: "He taught."

# Moment 3

*John*

It was a normal Thursday evening when the phone rang, informing me of a colicked horse on the way. My own horse had colicked a few weeks ago, and there was no one within four hours of Lamesa who could do a colic surgery. My horse died. I decided then and there that I was gonna learn to do a colic surgery on a horse and save horses for other people who couldn't make it four hours to a surgeon.

I always wanted to do colic surgeries. I knew they were very difficult and required a level of expertise that West Texas had not known before. It was more than just a decision on my part. It required learning many things that most veterinarians were not willing to attempt. But I was determined, and here was my chance.

John was sixteen years old. He was a horse that was used for disabled and mentally handicapped children to ride as a type of therapy and a chance for the human-animal bond to be established. I did not take my responsibility in this case lightly. I had been studying and honing my skill for weeks to be ready if the moment came that colic surgery was needed. Oh, it was more than weeks; it was years. I had paid close attention all through school, knowing that someday, I was going to be a surgeon. I felt as if the part of Texas I was eventually going to call my home was left hanging when it came to colic problems. This was not just a spur-of-the-moment decision; it was part of my mission to bring the best veterinary care to the horses of West Texas that veterinary medicine allowed.

Here it was. My first colic surgery. And it was on a horse that dozens of disabled kids loved deeply. I told Jenny, the owner of the horse, that

I had not done this before and that there were people four hours away who were better at it than I was. She looked at John as he suffered there and then looked back at me. She told me to do my best. She didn't think John would make it four more hours.

I went to work. I called in my friends and technicians, and we brought our talents and hopes together to work a miracle on ol' John. It was incredibly tough. John had an enterolith lodged in his transverse colon. That is one of the few pieces of horse guts that cannot be exteriorized to the outside and worked on. I found the thing quickly, but I had no idea how to cut that piece of gut open and remove the enterolith without contaminating the entire abdomen.

I went to work, did my best to figure out a way to get that four-pound petrified turd out of there. I blocked off other segments of bowel with huck towels and lap sponges. Remember, I could not even see what I was working on. In fact, the mineralized turd was stuck in a segment of bowel that was about three feet away from the incision I had made in the skin of John's belly. It was a full arm's length deep in the abdomen, and there was no way to see it. I could only feel it.

I could feel the pressure of numerous disabled children on my shoulders. I could feel the eyes of everyone in the room watching me and wondering if there was any possible way to get such a concretion out of the bowel of an aged horse without killing him with contamination. But there was no way I was going to give in to the pressure. Ol' John was going to live to be ridden again by those who loved him, and I was going to see to it.

I cut that bowel open deep within John and removed that four-pound stone from somewhere so dark and far away that it was almost as if it was another world. The blockage was gone, and the bowels were free to move again. But how was I going to sew up an eight-inch incision in a piece of bowel three feet away that I could not see? Oh man, huge pressure.

I had seen Dr. Deyhle suture things he couldn't see before. He had showed me how to use my hands without instruments as a tool to close tissue. I went to work. I put around fifty sutures in a piece of bowel that I never saw. I worked until my forearms were cramped up and aching and then worked some more. Finally, it was done. I closed the muscle and skin of the abdomen. I told Jenny that things were up to God now, and it was gonna be a tough journey to see if John lived.

I do about 150 colic surgeries a year now. I have done that many surgeries for lots of years. But John was my first. I watched him roll away from our clinic about two weeks later and thanked God that he had lived. I will never really know how he did live. There is no reason he should have. I was just beginning to figure out how to do that surgery, and I started with one of the hardest presentations there is.

I really don't know how long John lived. But I do know he lived for many, many years. He had several complications as time went by, but we managed to keep him going. He was one tough rascal. Serendipity may have been manipulating that moment in order to allow me the resolve to continue on learning how to do a colic surgery. A huge number of disabled children rode that old saint after he had surgery. They learned how superneato horses are because John didn't die on that Thursday.

I found confidence in John that pushed me on to learn more and become better. I studied hard and worked tirelessly to get to the point that I felt confident, no matter what the cause of colic was. It all started on a Thursday night, on a horse that was just too tough to give up. It was one of those moments that made all the difference. And I can thank Jenny and John for giving me a chance to embark on a part of my career that would ultimately lead to thousands of horses not dying when, by all indications, they should have.

&#8667;&#8728;&#8666;

I posted that story about John on the clinic Facebook page, and a few hours later, I found this under the comments. It is a sweet thing for Jenny to say, and it is why everyone at that clinic works so hard.

Wow...have been wiping tears from this for an hour now...I'm Jenny...John's owner...Bo is more than a small-town vet as you all know! He called me "Sunshine" and wished me happy birthday...even though it never was my real birthday! I can never say *thank you* enough for what he did that day! For you see..."John" was my main man! I had based my entire Angels on Horseback Therapeutic Riding program around his expertise! John, by the way, was actually twenty-one years old when this happened... Now that just makes Bo's story even better! No horse that age should have survived, much less been operated on in the first place. But when you have a horse you have been with since he was five years and gone through so much, you do what is needed to keep him alive! John was one of "those" horses that were one in a million! He knew his job was to help the kids I put on his back...He would respond to them unlike anything you have ever seen before! Hundreds of challenged kids rode him over the years...There were at least two or three that spoke their first words on his back...His perfect demeanor and gait allowed a young bride-to-be to walk down the aisle of her wedding instead of in a wheelchair! So many successes I witnessed over those twelve years of doing therapy...That's why Bo knew what he had to do and did it with such grace! What he didn't tell you is this was done way before he had his awesome clinic and surgery bays he has now...just red-canvas tent walls with some track lighting and some great buddies and volunteers that showed up in full force, knowing the hard task ahead. Oh, did I mention that it was December 17, at 11:00 p.m., and it was seventeen degrees outside! When Bo stepped up on a box literally to bend into John's belly, you could only see the top of his Cinch jeans. Everyone was freezing, but when he came out and up with this four-pound football, I thought it was a joke...You all know how [he] jokes! But all I saw was him sweating profusely in seventeen-degree weather and rolling this "thing" on the ground...That's when I fell to my knees and started praying harder! Not just for John but also for God to guide his hands on sewing him back up! I only tell these extra details because Bo is too modest, and that's why we all love him so much! He goes beyond the normal things and feels the customers' pain and makes you feel like you are his only priority in the world! I'm so glad he took the chance to start his colic surgery expertise on

John that cold night! John did therapy another four years and he lived his life out on my family's farm in Petersburg under the careful watch of my brother, Sid, until his death at thirty years old! And it wasn't from colic...just old age! Thank you again, Bo Brock, for everything you did and for not letting John die on that Thursday!

*six*
# Dogs

# Moment 1

*Buddy*

A dog that lives at a veterinary clinic quite possibly enjoys the best of all lifestyles in the canine world. Think about it: it has a built-in health-care policy; it gets to meet every dog in town; it gets to bark at and chase cattle as they are loaded and unloaded, and—maybe best of all—it gets to eat the leftovers.

That's right: nothing better for a carnivore than meat. All those body parts left over at the end of the day at the clinic—there are horns from dehorning, placentas from birthing, hooves from horseshoeing, and, perhaps best of all, oysters from castrations.

Buddy was our first clinic dog. He was an eighty-pound Airedale terrier that never knew anything other than the life of a vet-clinic dog. I think he may still hold the world record for the number of mountain oysters eaten in one day: fifty-four. Makes those guys who swallowed goldfish in their college days seem like nothing.

I decided that Buddy needed a bit of culture, so I began taking him to obedience school when he was about a year old. This, of course, was not his favorite thing to do. It involved discipline and dedication, two qualities that running free in the clinic had not instilled in him. At first, just the sight of that leash made his tail go between his legs and elicited a most pitiable facial expression.

The lessons were every Thursday night at the livestock barn. It was a group class, with about fifteen dogs at each meeting. Buddy learned to sit, stay, and come. He advanced to lying down and following at the perfect distance. Learning quickly and remembering well, Buddy became a star.

He exceeded my expectations until about the fifth lesson, when he seemed to have a lapse of reason. It was as though he suddenly forgot everything he had learned.

At the start of each class, we would all walk around in circles, one behind the other; it was sort of a warm-up to get the dogs tuned up and to realize that we were about to have a lesson.

This fifth Thursday night found Buddy with no sense at all. He fought the leash, tried to sniff all the girl dogs, growled at the boy dogs, and was driving me crazy, forcing me to pull on the choke chain with a bit more force than usual. That extra pressure made him cough and gag a bit, enough so that he stopped and heaved up some of the day's prizes from the clinic.

Picture this: a cold winter night in a fair barn in Lamesa, fifteen dogs walking in a circle, a steaming pile of fresh mountain oysters, no time to stop the parade to dispose of them, and the next dog in line...a two-pound Yorkie.

I think you know where this story is going.

I heard the woman scream and say, "Oh my!" when she saw what her Yorkie had in his mouth. That's right, the two-pound dog was carrying a mountain oyster almost as big as he was. It was hanging out both sides of his mouth, and he was proud as a peacock.

It was then I decided that a Yorkie probably wouldn't be a good clinic dog. Any attempt to remove the oyster from its mouth was met with serious growls and a display of tiny teeth. The owner was beside herself. She had no idea what it was or where it had come from, and I was not about to tell her.

We finally stopped the entire process and went about removing Yorkie from the mountain oyster. It took quite a bit of work, but we finally got it away from him and resumed the lesson.

As we marched back around toward the smoking pile, I was able to cover it with dirt to prevent another episode on the following lap.

I bet that to this day that woman has no idea what her pet was gnawing on or where it came from.

And unless she reads this, she'll never learn it from me.

### Buddy Eulogy

It is true that a veterinarian has to see the world through the eyes of an animal much of the time. For the past eight years, I have seen the world through the eyes of a big ol' Airedale dog named Buddy. He came to the clinic as a four-pound puppy and grew into an eighty-five-pound teddy bear that greeted every dog that came into the clinic with a friendly fanny sniff.

He has given more than his weight in blood for transfusions and has been a part of saving countless lives. He can pick out the lesion on the animal before I ever start doing surgery. If it is in the back, he will stand there and watch until he is pitched the results. Buddy has been friends with three dogcatchers and knows most everyone in Dawson and the surrounding counties.

But what I thank Buddy most for is allowing me to see the world though a different set of eyes. He has shown me people through the eyes of an animal and animals through the eyes of someone who truly cares. Sometimes it is hard to understand how much people care for a pet. Buddy revealed to me the bond that makes people care so deeply for a critter. Because of him, I can cry when an elderly woman loses her best friend, a poodle she has had for fourteen years. Because of him, I go to extremes to make those last few months or years comfortable when a person has no one else to talk to all day long but an overweight Schnauzer. Because I see the world through his eyes, I can see how people need pets to give them sunshine.

When the world has collapsed, and there's no love at all, there will still be the love of a dog. They just don't know how to do otherwise. I've seen stoic, old cowboys sob over the loss of dogs that helped them work by day and gave them smiles, stories, and a listening ear. I've seen children's faces light up over a puppy that would love without conditions.

On Father's Day, at five o'clock, Buddy died. I feel lost every time I castrate a horse and there is no Buddy to talk to about the rewards. I miss his powerful head rubbing against my hand for an occasional scratching. I've told stories of Buddy's adventures to six classes of veterinarian students at Texas A&M and in several states. He had a personality that was wonderful. He had the patience of Job with small children and other animals. He loved people, and I know he loved me.

We will miss you, Buddy. Thanks for the sunshine.

# Moment 2

*Ennis*

Having a veterinarian for a daddy doesn't make you any more of a vet than standing in a garage makes you a car. But my daughters have been asked questions about sick animals their entire lives, as if somehow my going to veterinary school was genetically transferred to them.

Nubbin is buddies with my oldest daughter, Emili, and her husband, Garrett. He got the name because when he was a kid, some accident claimed the end of his thumb, and the nickname "Nubbin" was the outcome. This fella, Nubbin, is a farmer and a redneck kind of individual. He's the last person you would ever expect to have a Basset hound.

Nubbin called Emili in a bit of a fizz one night recently because his Basset hound, Ennis, was making more noise than usual. Basset hounds make noise. And making more noise than usual means way too much noise.

"I don't know what is wrong with him. He just sets with his legs out to the side on the kitchen floor and howls like something is bothering him. Could you come have a look at him, Emili, and see if som'in' is wrong?" was the message my daughter got from Nubbin that night.

So Dr. Emili and Garrett made the trek to the homestead of Nubbin to check out the possible causes of kitchen settin' in a Basset hound. When they arrived, they found things just as Nubbin had described them. Ennis was setting on the kitchen floor with his nose pointed in the air, howling like a wolf. The sound penetrated the walls and the entire area around the house. Ennis was in misery.

Emili went to work. She asked how long it had been going on. Nubbin informed her since early that morning. She asked if Ennis had had a change of diet. Nope, was all Nubbin had to say to that. She asked if he was current on his shots, if he had gotten out of the yard, if he had been vomiting or had diarrhea, if he was coughing or sneezing, if he was limping when he walked, if there were any fleas or ticks, if anything at all might suggest why Ennis had the blues. None of the questions turned up even a clue.

Finally, Dr. Emili began the physical exam on ol' Ennis. She looked in his ears, his eyes, his mouth, his nose...nothing. She began touching the skin on his back and evaluating his skin. Ennis was a mostly white Basset hound with a few patches of black dispersed here and there. Nothing on the top of the dog revealed the source of his misery.

Finally, Emili rolled that critter over and began to analyze his belly. There was the answer just as plain as day. Ennis's skin was bright red on his underside, but especially on his scrotum. Not knowing what the cause could be, Emili suggested that maybe he had lain down on his stomach on something caustic.

To this, Nubbin replied, "Oh no, I know what happened. He always sleeps lying on his back. And yesterday I left him out in the backyard all day while I was gone. I bet he sunburned his belly and balls while he was asleep."

This, of course, started son-in-law Garrett to laughing. And I mean laughing. Laughing to the point that he was unable to speak for ten minutes. Here is ol' Ennis the Basset resting his sunburned scrotum on the cool tile floor in the kitchen and howling with either pleasure or pain to the point that Dr. Emili was called in to investigate.

"What do you do for sunburned balls on a Basset?" asked Nubbin. "I can't sleep at night if he keeps this up."

Being the clever daughter of a veterinarian, Emili never missed a beat in her response. "You will have to go down to the store and get some aloe vera gel and rub the skin of his scrotum down with it, or he will bark all night!"

I have this picture in my mind of redneck Nubbin rubbin' aloe vera juice all over the scrotum of a Basset hound named Ennis in order to find enough peace to sleep that night. I am like Garrett. It makes me laugh hard for ten minutes.

# Moment 3

*Josh*

Josh was a fuzzy, gray dog with eyes that bulged out like Marty Feldman's, and a raging under bite. I estimated him at about twenty-five pounds and somewhere around fifteen years old as I observed him tucked under his owner's left arm while she stood in the waiting room.

She had that indescribable look about her that screamed she was a waitress at a diner, and her face was torqued into an obviously worried expression that I assumed was the result of some problem with Josh.

She stood there tapping her toe, waiting her turn to check in, holding Josh safely in that left arm, and a white plastic Walmart sack with something stuffed in it in her right hand. I had been in Lamesa for only a few days, and I knew almost no one. Every client who came in the door was a brand-new relationship to develop, and I looked at each one of them as a new friend.

When we met in the exam room, I went to work examining Josh. I took his temperature...normal. I listened to the heart and lungs...normal. I looked in the eyes, ears, and throat...normal. I felt all the lymph nodes and skin...normal. All the while, the waitress-looking woman was jabbering about how worried she was about him.

I went into the next phase of the exam, the history. Josh was actually sixteen years old, and he was looking a little arthritic. I began quizzing this worried woman about symptoms: Has he been vomiting? No.

Has he had any diarrhea? No.

Has he stopped eating or drinking? No.

Does he cough or wheeze? No.

Is he stumbling around or acting crippled? No.

I was just about out of questions and had not even a clue as to why she was so worried about ol' Josh. I was about to volley another round of questions when the waitress-looking woman reached into the Walmart sack, pulled out a grungy-looking stuffed bear, and handed it to me.

I held it in my hand and examined it. It was a gross-looking little bear with matted hair. It looked like some low-quality, grade-B stuffed animal that came from the carnie row at the county fair. I was waiting to hear how this stuffed animal had anything to do with the problem at hand, but she just stood there and looked at me as if I was holding the obvious answer to the entire world's health problems.

Still not a word. Just a raised-eyebrow expression that seemed to suggest I had no idea what to do as a veterinarian if that stuffed animal did not reveal the problem. I began looking closely at it again during the uncomfortably long pause. Maybe I was missing something. I looked to see if maybe it had button eyes and one of them was missing. Maybe Josh had eaten it...no. I looked to see if it was chewed or torn. Maybe he had eaten some stuffing...no.

Finally, after what seemed like five minutes, she began to speak.

"That is Sweetie Pie, the stuffed bear. Josh humps that bear two to three times a day and has for the last fifteen years. I am extremely worried about Josh because he hasn't humped it one time in the last two weeks. I am completely sure something very bad is wrong with him."

I released my grip on the bear, all except the thumb and first finger, and gently handed it back to her.

What the heck was I supposed to do about that? Dang, Josh was something like a ninety-year-old human. I was not ninety yet, but I was guessing ninety-year-old dudes weren't doing much twice-a-day humping.

I was brand-new in town. I wanted people to like me as a doctor and tell their friends to come see Dr. Brock. I could tell by looking that the woman was not going to have any sort of respect for me as the new doctor in town if I didn't get Josh back to twice a day BID humping. I was scanning my brain for any information they gave me back in veterinary school that would help me out a bit here...nothing.

*Come on, Bo. Think of something here, buddy. You can fix this! Use your common sense if you can't find any science.* These thoughts were rushing through my brain as I stood there trying to look like I saw this problem all the time.

I had seen the commercials for low testosterone on television, and all those fellas seemed to be totally happy after a few doses of the hormone. So I decided to give ol' Josh a little shot of testosterone in the muscle. Not so much as to cause some type of health problem; just enough to make Sweetie Pie look as beautiful to him as she did fifteen years ago. I had no idea if it would help, but this woman did not buy my story about a ninety-year-old man when I tried that first.

About a week passed, and the waitress-looking woman called. She was as happy as could be. She informed me that I was the best veterinarian Lamesa had ever seen. She went on to say that sometimes he humped it four times a day now.

# Moment 4

## *Tripod*

The leg was broken beyond repair.

It is amazing the trauma that can occur when a dog is struck by a car. What made it even worse was the fact that this heeler dog apparently had no owner. He just wandered up into a young couple's yard in Lamesa with multiple fractures in one hind leg and a look of despair in his eyes.

Despite what you might think, the world is full of caring people. This couple showed up at my veterinary clinic with broken hearts and a request to make him a three-legged dog. It was obvious to them that there was no fixing the leg, and, without surgery, the dog would suffer and eventually die.

Dr. Smith went to work. He is a remarkable surgeon. After a couple of hours, the dog woke up with three good legs and a second chance at life. He stayed around the clinic for several days while recovering, and we all became attached to his gentle and happy nature.

It always takes a dog a while to get used to having three legs. What a confusing moment it must be when they wake up from surgery and look down to see a missing limb. I often wonder what they are thinking the first time an ear itches and the normal thought process that leads to a thorough scratching results in nothing but an ear that still itches.

On their first trip outside after such surgery, male dogs usually spend some time looking at the now-missing leg and a tree that needs marking. Their faces take on a puzzled look, and the dance is on. They move from one side to the other, trying to figure out how this new situation is going to affect one of their proudest moments.

This dog took to three legs like a duck to water. In no time, he was bouncing around the clinic looking as agile as he was with all four wheels. As with most major surgeries, there is always a chance of infection. The animal doesn't know to leave the incision alone and often will lick and chew on the area. This dog managed to chew the stitches out twice, and each time we would go back and repair the damage. Finally, after a couple of weeks, the stitches came out, and the animal was ready to go back to his new home as "Tripod," the luckiest dog in Lamesa.

It was sad to see him go, but we knew that his new owners would take good care of him and we would see him from time to time for vaccinations. Little did we know as we waved good-bye that his story was just beginning.

I talked to the owners a week or so later, and they said he was doing fine. There was a little exudate coming from the scar as it healed, but otherwise, everything was going well. They just loved him.

Time went by. New patients came in, and old ones faded into memory. We had filed Tripod in our memory banks, and were busy making new memories, when a voice at the other end of the telephone one day held a surprise.

"You're never going to believe what happened," the caller said. "About four months ago, my dog ran away, and I just assumed he was dead. I looked high and low for him. He was the best dog I ever had. I just about had given up hope, when last night he showed up at home and in good shape.

"Well, not exactly in perfect shape," the caller said. "I think I need to bring him in. He is eating and drinking OK, but you're not gonna believe this. When he left, he had four legs, and now...well, now, he has just three. Not only that, it has already haired over, and he barely has a scar. What do you figure happened?"

What kind of emotions must have been in this man's head as he soaked up the reunion? How does a dog disappear for a month and then show up with a perfectly amputated leg?

We told him the story and called the young couple.

Now Tripod is back in his original home and probably living the most amazing life of any dog in Dawson County.

# Moment 5

*A Tribute to Weenie Dogs*

We said good-bye to the last of their two weenie dogs today. I felt their tears as the black one fell asleep for the last time. Nearly a year of poor health was ending, and with it came the tender memories that would be too sensitive to touch for a while. Some people would say that it was just a dog, but I beg to differ, and so would the dog's elderly owners. Those of us who are younger may be wise to see how the sunshine years hold a tribute to weenie dogs.

The weenie dogs gave their owners something to care for—they were living creatures that still need their owners for guidance and the basics of life. Yet more than this, the dogs gave them meaning, meaning that carried over from years of raising children and grandchildren. You cannot just turn those emotions off as time changes its definitions of wisdom and usefulness.

They gave stories to share with one another as the retirement years set in. Adventures hung in the air for hours, and short legs carried long backs into the mischievousness of puppyhood. Each new trick was story material for the next phone call from family. Lap time was special; not a bump or change in skin texture went unnoticed.

And what about the exercise? The black dog was paralyzed in the hindquarters for almost eleven months. Improvement was slow, but it was coming. The surgery had been a success, and a good prognosis depended on a lot of physical therapy at home. Imagine that! Eleven months of walking...and exercising...and moving those legs...and swimming that critter in the bathtub...and carrying it outside...and tucking it into bed. Kinda makes you wonder who got the most exercise. Kinda makes you wonder, would you have exercised at all?

No disappointment. This love is unconditional. So what if you go to bed at eight thirty? They'll be more than happy to stay right beside the bed until 5:00 a.m., when you start the next day. So what if you keep the house at eighty-eight degrees year-round? They've never known it to be different. So what if you drive twenty-five miles per hour on the interstate? They just love going for rides. So what if you tell the same story over and over? They love it as much the last time as they did the first.

Inside of me is a huge tribute to weenie dogs. I've seen their effect. I've laughed at those stories. I've helped you notice every bump and change in skin texture. I've monitored that exercise program. And I've seen that love in your eyes as you held a precious friend in your lap.

When the world has collapsed and there is no love at all, there will still be the love of a dog. They just don't know how to do otherwise.

*seven*

# Bovines

# Moment 1

### Big White Bull

I was running away as fast as I could when the big white bull's head made contact with my right bun. I remember being surprised by its softness as it moved up the back of my thigh. The softness didn't last long, though. It was quickly replaced with incredible force—the kind that makes you suddenly feel small, like a little kid playing with Dad or a skier being pulled out of the water by a motorboat.

A false sense of security had lured me into the predicament at hand. Most bulls will either run you out of the pen to begin with or put up with you to the end. Not this one! He started off just fine and then turned into the devil. He had decided it was time to rid the pen of the scoundrel veterinarian who kept touching his recently acquired boo-boo. He had put up with it for three or four minutes, but now the vet had to go.

His left horn hooked my overstuffed wallet. The connection must have caused his adrenal gland to contract, fueling him with a burst of energy. The weight ratio of bull to man was ten to one—his two thousand pounds to my two hundred—and was readily apparent as I went flying.

My next sensation was almost pleasant. Weightlessness is most surely more enjoyable when it is not interrupted by thoughts of "How high am I going to go?" and "Where am I going to land?" My legs and arms flailed, fruitlessly grabbing at air, as I tried to position myself to absorb the landing in the least painful manner. Midair calculations told me that if the fence was five feet tall, I must have been ten or twelve feet in the air as I sailed over it. I was much higher than the cab of my pickup. In fact, I was going over the cab of my pickup.

Let's see, what was in the back of my pickup? I was trying to remember because my calculations had me traveling right over the cab and landing in the bed.

Then I remembered: pig feed! I had just loaded eight fifty-pound bags of pig feed into the bed of the truck, and they were, for once, actually lying perfectly flat. I was thanking myself for taking a little extra time to put them in the truck in an organized manner as the bed of the truck came into view.

Oh my! I had forgotten about the shovel! There it was, sharp side up and poised to strike like a hissing snake. It was the last thing I had put in and was, of course, on top of the soft sacks of pig feed. My hands and head were coming in first. All I would have to do was give the shovel a quick shove and then roll over on my shoulder, and all would be well. I could hear the spectators making those sounds that people make when something awful is about to happen—a gasp coupled with a sudden inhale.

Thank goodness, the shovel had slid forward a bit when I stopped the truck. This left me about two feet of space to reach my hands out and push the shovel toward the cab. Of course, I missed. However, the motion to push the shovel caused me to roll up into a neat ball, which was the form I took as I landed, wedged between the tailgate and the last feed sack.

The crowd moved in to see if I was alive. I let out a few moans as I began to uncoil, assessing my body for damage. My head had narrowly missed the shovel. And as far as I could tell, everything still moved and was still attached. I lay there for a minute, listening as the group reenacted the event and gabbed about the luck of landing on that pig feed. I pondered why anyone would go to school for eight years to get to do something like this.

We wound up taking the bull to the clinic because I assured them that my time in the pen was over. It was just another day in the life of a small-town veterinarian.

# Moment 2

### One-Eyed Cow

S top and think about it for a moment: How big is a fifteen-hundred-pound cow? Oh, it's about as large as the entire offensive line for the Dallas Cowboys. It weighs as much as half a car or about five refrigerators. That's a lot of mass to be driven by such a small brain.

Discovering the force of such an animal is almost a rite of passage; all budding veterinarians must be reminded how much a cow weighs. No matter how strong you think you are, you are not stronger than a fifteen hundred-pound cow.

This particular veterinary student had been looking forward to the ranch trip for days. When he found out that we were going to spend an entire day at a ranch, palpating cattle, he was on cloud nine. Judging by his enthusiasm, I guessed he had very little experience with it. The forecast called for a high of around 105 degrees with little to no wind. So, we would be sticking our arms up the fannies of seven hundred to eight hundred cows in the bottom of a 105-degree canyon with no breeze for about twelve hours.

We had been at it for about five hours. The air was filled with dust that became intensely plastered to the continuous supply of sweat dripping from each of us. It was almost like dipping catfish in eggs and milk just before rolling it in cornmeal. My job was to palpate the cows for pregnancy and sort the open ones from the bred ones. The macho veterinary student was helping with the vaccinations and occasionally palpating.

He was doing well, the big muscled-up fellow. I'm guessing he could bench-press about three hundred pounds. This might have given him a false sense of security, I would later conclude.

Midway through our day, the one-eyed cow came barreling into the chute, slinging snot and high kicking with both back feet. I just love this kind of cow—they can only see what is happening on one side, so they are on a constant hunt for something sneaking up on them from the other side.

All of the cows at this particular ranch were a bit snakey, but this one-eyed one was too much. You learn to get in and out of these wild ones in a hurry. I palpated her; thank goodness, she was open. The cowboy hollered, "Open," and the student ran to the end of the alley to open the gate into the cull pen.

He just kinda stood there as she went by him on her blind side. As she made the turn, he must have come into view of her good eye, because she turned into a fifteen-hundred-pound veterinary student magnet. Her head went down, and snot started flying. After you have seen a few cows go into the "I am going to pulverize you" dance, climbing the nearest fence quickly becomes an involuntary response.

I guess my student had not seen that particular dance before because he made no attempt to scramble. He just kinda stood there and watched her heading straight for him. I'm not sure, but I think he figured she would stop and run away before she reached him. He was wrong! She started slinging him around like a rag doll.

I could see the thoughts running through his mind as she got her head under his fanny and pitched him effortlessly into the air. I could almost see the dialogue bubbles like a cartoon: "Bench-pressing three hundred pounds is meaningless right now...I wish I didn't wear my pants so tight...One-eyed cows are not afraid of veterinary students... Now I know why everyone scrambled for the fences...I bet Dr. Brock will put this in his column."

We got there just about the time she got tired of whoopin' on him. It was a pretty good pounding, judging from his torn-off britches and his bloodied nose. We got him in the pickup just in time to watch him turn white and pass out.

## Chapter Seven

I'm pretty sure he will never forget that day. He learned what the pulverizing dance looks like; he learned that it's not sissy to climb a fence; he learned how to finish working cattle in a nearly nonexistent pair of britches; and most of all, he learned that no matter how strong you think you are, you are not stronger than a cow.

*eight*

Goats

# Moment 1

*Frustration*

Have you ever been through one of those days when everything that happens just gets on your nerves? You know, those days when even the things that should deliver a smile kinda make your teeth grit between the lips of a forced grin? Well, when those days come upon me, I think back on the most frustrated critter I have ever known, and it seems to make whatever made me tense seem so incredibly small.

We called him Gomer because that is what he was. During the process of embryo transfer, we must know when the goats are in the right stage of heat in order to know if the synchronization of the donor and recipient are correct. In order to find this out, we need a boy goat. This boy goat must fulfill a few essential requirements. First, he must not be too big. This is because we don't want him to hurt the females or us. Second, he must be able to detect a female goat that is in heat. This means he must be intact. Third, and most importantly, he must not be able to breed with the female. So how is one to accomplish all these things?

Years ago, someone came up with the "great idea" to create a gomer goat. This is done by surgically moving his "boy part" to where it exits on the side instead of straight ahead. This fulfills all of the requirements. It leaves the goat intact, yet it prevents the billy goat from getting the female pregnant.

So, we went about making one of these creatures. The surgery is not hard. After the procedure, we let the gomer goat have about two weeks to recover, and then we fasten a harness that has some colored marking chalk on it between his front legs, and when he mounts the female, he will color her back and miss her "girl part." This is how we know when the female goat is ready to be used in the embryo-transfer procedure.

I must say that it is a very good idea and works extremely well for everyone involved except Gomer. You should have seen the look on his face the first time he mounted a prime female specimen and saw his "boy part" come scooting out the side. Not only that, but you should have seen the look on the female's face when she saw it. He hopped off her and just froze. I think he suddenly realized why he had been hitting himself in the ear with tee tee for the last two weeks. He looked to that side and then to the other. I think he was checking to see if he had two. He jumped up in the air and then ran about, making a tremendous "mad goat" sound. He went over and butted a couple of young males as if to make sure it wasn't they who had done it. And then, as if he thought perhaps he had awakened from a bad dream, he went over and tried the female again. The result was the same. He just stood there and looked at it. It looked to me as if his expression was saying, "Can you believe this? Of all the bad luck. I went to sleep, and when I woke up, my 'boy part' was pointing east. *What am I going to do?*"

The breeding season went on, and eventually we were having to get the goats up every day to check them. This was a difficult task. There was a fellow in the clinic one day watching us who suggested that we get a dog to help round them up. I told him that ol' Gomer, there, wouldn't put up with a dog in his pen.

The man replied, "That little goat couldn't hurt my dog."

So, I said, "Bring him on."

And he did.

By now, Gomer was frustrated. He had tried every way possible to work around the problem. He would stand on one foot, mount her from the side, put both front feet on one side, and lie on his back. He would try to talk the female into moving her fanny over. Nothing would work. At times, he would be surrounded by thirty or forty goats in heat, and all he could do was mount and watch. His frustrations accumulated until he was just downright mean.

When this fellow showed up with his dog, it was quite a sight to behold. He told the dog to go get the goats. This dog took off like a shot.

## Chapter Eight

It ran around to the back and into Gomer. Ol' Gomer tore that dog up like a sow's bed. Gomer hung his horn under the collar of the dog and carried it around, butting it on everything in sight. The dog was yipping and screaming, and for just a moment, I thought I saw Gomer smile.

The breeding season came to an end, and we no longer needed Gomer. Of course, we moved his boy part back to the intended position. I have often wondered about him. If he is still alive and happily breeding nannies, what do you think he tells the boys down at the barbershop about the year he spent in Lamesa?

∂∽⟨

### Frustration: A Mini-Epilogue

Brock Veterinary Clinic has a group of loiterers. It is a club made up mostly of retired farmers, retired military dudes, schoolteachers from the past, and a few people who just come down on their days off to hang out and watch.

I am not sure how or when this loiterer group got started, but it evolved into a group that almost always had one member at the clinic. Very few moments in the day passed without one or two of them standing around watching for what might happen next. Sometimes they get in the way, but most of the time, they just hang back and give commentary on what is going on.

This bothers some people, but it really doesn't bother me too much. I like to hear their old war stories and what they are gonna say next about whatever it is that may be happening.

The membership hit an all-time high the year Gomer lived at the clinic. These old dudes thought that was the funniest thing they had ever seen. They would show up in the mornings with lawn chairs and coffee and set outside the pasture watching poor ol' Gomer swing and miss. Every time, it would bring a roar of laughter from the geriatric section. They never seemed to tire of watching the process and seeing what Gomer was going to try next to get things to line up. About twice a day, they would come find me and tell me about the latest thing Gomer had done. Oh my, they absolutely loved it. I often wondered if it was because none of their "boy parts" worked anymore and they could relate to a billy goat that wanted to but just couldn't get it done.

It turned out to be a really good thing for me. By the end of the day, they could tell me every nanny that was in heat and how long she had been standing. I sure didn't have time to stand there all day and make sure the marking chalk was accurate in showing which critter was ready to have an embryo. We did a really good job of embryo transferring because of those old rascals.

*nine*

Pigs

# Pigs

It was a lush backyard. I mean lush.

There were trees and vines and ivy and shrubs and bushes and fountains—and a potbellied pig.

That's right, one large pig called this paradise home. She was living in the perfect pig world. She had everything a pig could want. There was a muddy wallow, soft soil to root in, shade, plenty of food, and all the attention a pig could want.

My mission was to vaccinate the critter for all those "bad pig diseases" that might sneak into the yard. It was my last call of the day, and I brought along my five-year-old daughter.

We entered through the house, and the hog owner took us to the pig paradise she called a backyard. I had to stop for a minute and think how wonderful it must be to live in this yard. As I stood there absorbing the surroundings, my eyes fell on Prudence. She was sunning in a mudhole next to the forest that crept along the back fence. She was framed in ivy that was growing around the trees.

"Is she hard to catch?" was the first thing out of my mouth as I pondered how I was going to give three shots to a free-roaming pig.

"Oh no," replied the owner. "She just loves people and will come when I call her."

I figured she would come for a belly scratching, but what was she going to do when I stuck an eighteen-gauge needle in her neck? How was I going to hold on to a slick, muddy hog that could probably make more noise than a 747? I wasn't too worried. This pig was so fat that I figured I could outrun her. Maybe I could just turn her over on her back like a turtle.

Sure enough, the woman gave a sweet-sounding yodel. "Prudence, come here, baby," she called, and the pig hopped out of the mud and came waddling toward the three of us. We petted her for a while and heard all the stories the woman had gathered over the years of having a pig in the backyard.

I gotta admit, the pig was pretty cute. She grunted and oinked as we scratched those hard-to-reach places. I decided that the time was right to slip the first injection gently into her neck muscle. I tried the "sneak it in" approach. The moment the needle went through her skin, she turned into the fastest-moving animal I had ever seen! In fact, her reaction time startled me so much that I let go of the syringe and needle. As bad luck would have it, the needle had gone in far enough that the entire syringe and needle were still in the pig.

Off she went, heading for the cover of the forest and mud with me hot on her trail. Just before we hit the heavy vegetation, the syringe fell off the needle, leaving only one and a half inches of stainless hypodermic needle embedded deep in the muscle of her neck. This was a problem. The weight of the syringe would have surely pulled the whole thing loose from the pig, but now there was nothing to weight the end of the needle. It was in there to stay.

We ran through the forest, dove past the mud holes, tangled and wrestled in the ivy, and darted around the storage house; this pig knew every avenue the yard had to offer.

I was quickly deciding that the pig was not as slow as I had first anticipated. I would hear my five-year-old daughter laughing and saying, "Daddy, you look funny running all bent over like that!"

Maybe this is why I couldn't catch Prudence. Have you ever tried running full speed, bent over at the waist, while extending your arms? It is not easy, and I am sure it made me look like an even bigger nerd than I am.

I stopped and decided to try a new tactic. Running was not going to work. The owner of the pig was saying, "Oh my! *Oh my!*" over and over. What a predicament—a panicked owner, a lightning-fast pig, and a laughing five-year-old! I was determined not to let this pig get the best of me!

## Chapter Nine

Prudence finally settled back down in her mudhole. The problem was, if I moved toward her, she stood up and assumed the sprinter's starter position. So, I would back off a little, and she would lie back down. I was all the way across the yard from her and could see no way of sneaking up on her. She had a good view of the entire yard from her position in the mud.

It was then I noticed a giant beach ball next to my right foot. It was Prudence's favorite toy. I decided to use it as a decoy to hide behind. I lay on my stomach behind the beach ball and gradually belly crawled, behind the cover of the ball, across the yard toward the needle-pierced pig.

The tension mounted as I approached her. The closer I got, the slower I progressed. I had narrowed the gap to about five feet without drawing her attention. I could feel the sweat beading up on my forehead as I anticipated the moment.

I leaped from behind the ball like a cheetah starting the chase. She didn't have a chance to move. I grabbed that needle out of her neck and held my hands up like a cowboy who had just tied a calf. Cheers erupted from the laughing five-year-old and the stressed-out hog owner.

We came to a mutual agreement that the risk of catching a contagious hog disease in the middle of town was minimal and decided not to try vaccinating the speedy Prudence ever again.

*ten*

Cats

# Cats

The cat's name was Whoops, and it fit the rascal perfectly. He arrived in a pet carrier and would hiss and slap at the cage door if anyone even looked in his direction.

Most veterinarians will agree that there is almost nothing as dangerous as an angry cat. They have four feet, a mouthful of sharp teeth, and they are lightning fast.

Mother of Whoops kindly said that she would leave him in the cage, and we could get him out when it was time for his surgery.

Whoops was about to undergo a declaw procedure. That's what happens when you are a house cat and decide that the arm of the leather couch is a good place to sharpen your claws.

Whoops had taken to this hobby about a month earlier. Now that the old couch was ruined, Mother of Whoops had ordered a new one. The claws had to go before it arrived. I don't particularly like this surgery. It seems a bit drastic to me, but I guess it's better than putting the cat to sleep.

Let me give you a quick rundown of how we do it: We anesthetize the cat and then remove the claw from the end of each toe. We do it in just the right place to keep it from growing back but without affecting the animal's motility. After the claw is removed, we close the space with tissue adhesive (a fancy word for superglue) and wrap the paw with an antibiotic bandage. The cat usually is back to running around the house in a couple of days.

The surgery on Whoops went perfectly, and we put him back in the carrier before he woke up to prevent another wrestling match. I check on recovering surgical patients quite often, and in about an hour, he was hissing at me when I looked in on him. You know a cat is a bit on the mean side when he lies on his side on the carrier floor one hour after surgery and hisses at everyone who walks by.

Mother of Whoops came at the scheduled time to pick him up. I told her he did well and was waking in the peaceful environment of his carrier. She smiled as I carried Whoops to the car and seemed content that her new couch was safe.

About nine that night, the phone rang. It was Mother of Whoops, who sounded a bit worried. It seemed Whoops would not leave the cage.

She opened the carrier door and placed it in his room, assuming that when he felt like it, he would come out. It had been several hours, but he had stayed there, just as he was when she picked him up.

This alarmed me a bit, too. I couldn't imagine why he would not be awake and alert enough by now to walk. I asked her to meet me at the clinic, and we would have a look.

She handed the cage to me and sat in the waiting room. I went into the exam room and opened the cage door. There he was, hissing and still in the same position in which I left him hours earlier.

What could be wrong?

I had never heard of a cat being paralyzed in declaw surgery. Everything had gone well...

Then it dawned on me.

The tissue adhesive I'd used to close the surgical sites had exploded a bit when I opened it.

As I examined the hissing critter, it was apparent that some of it had gotten on the cat and in the carrier.

Whoops was glued to the carrier floor.

I gently reached under him and cut the hair that was holding him down. It must have been a larger explosion than I realized because he was stuck tight in several places.

He was up and moving—a happy cat—in no time.

I returned him to the owner and blushingly described what had happened. She was understanding and just glad that things turned out well.

All I could say about my miscue was...whoops!

*eleven*

# Birds

# Moment 1

## Ostrich

Have you ever had a closeup look at an ostrich? Do you have any idea how big those rascals really are?

The first time I ever saw one in the flesh was when the owners of a seven-foot-tall, 350-pound female ostrich called me for help. It seemed that the big bird had stepped on something and had a raging infection in her foot. The owners couldn't catch her. Actually, they were frightened to death of their own birds.

As I peered into a chicken-wire fortress, I noticed that the tall bird's boyfriend was in the same three-acre compound. He must have stood eight feet tall.

My assignment: enter the enclosure, wrestle down the giant creature, remove whatever might be stuck in her foot, give her a shot, treat the abscess—and do it all without help from the couple who owned her.

Oh, they were full of advice, but that was as far as it went. They were not about to touch anything.

Their constant stream of advice was the farthest thing from my mind as I sized up the situation.

The first thing I noticed was the size of the toes on that bird. The biggest one must have been seven inches long, with a rock-hard, razor-sharp toenail on the end. I realized that I should be more afraid of the feet than the head.

Then I saw the drumsticks. To carry around 350 pounds, you need big drumsticks. I guessed that this beast defended herself with her legs.

My next question was, which way does she kick? Does she strike backward like a horse or forward like a rooster? I went with the latter theory and decided I would just treat her like a big chicken.

When I entered the pen, much to my surprise, both ostriches just sidled up to me and started pecking on anything that was shiny, first my ring and then the button on top of my cap. This gave me a chance to size up the foot injury at close range. It was bad.

I realized that there was no way I was going to be able to pick up that foot. Every time I tried to touch it, she opened her mouth so wide that her face disappeared and gave a mighty hiss.

I left the pen and headed for a cell phone. I had no idea how to sedate an ostrich but figured that someone did. The guy on the phone had very little advice—just the correct dose of anesthetic, a chuckle, and a warning to "give the shot in the muscles of the breast."

I quickly discovered that I couldn't chase down an ostrich, even one with an abscessed foot, so I decided to hide behind a bush in a small gully, wait for her to come by, stick her with the injection, and wait for her to fall asleep.

Things were looking good.

The owners waved a food bowl outside the fence to attract the bird's attention. She saw it and headed that way, right toward my hiding spot. That's when I noticed that the gully was just deep enough that I wouldn't be at the right angle to reach the breast muscles.

By then, however, I was committed. I jumped on her, reached under her left wing, and gave the shot while my legs dangled off her right side. This bird was actually carrying me! None of me was touching the ground, and that made me uncomfortable. I hopped off and tumbled to a stop as the owners cheered me on.

That's when I saw him coming.

Oh yes, him. The once-docile male ostrich suddenly had become possessive of his girlfriend. He spread his white-tipped wings and came at me full of bad intentions. At the end of about ten running steps, I learned that you cannot climb chicken wire.

Things were getting desperate. There was no way I could outrun this guy. Nothing left to do but fight. I looked around for some sort of weapon—a stick, a rock, anything—with which to defend myself. Nothing.

I had no choice but to face him.

What would you have done? Without even thinking, I just braced myself and started yelling at him.

"Hey, get outta here!" came pouring out of my mouth as I waved my arms and kicked dirt.

That was all it took. He folded up and ran the other way as if he'd seen a ghost.

My heart was pounding, and I was shaking all over. All I could think as I trotted toward the gate that offered freedom was, *Eight years of school for that?*

The female bird responded well to treatment once we got the thorn out of her foot.

Those people didn't own ostriches much longer, as I recall.

As for me, I still have dreams about giant, white-winged birds chasing me around a chicken-wire pen I can't climb out of.

# Moment 2

### Mystery

The directions I held in my hand were leading me to a residential district in Lubbock, Texas. That would not have been a big deal were it not for the fact that I was on my way to visit a horse. I knew that people in a city residential area were likely to know as much about horses as I knew about submarines, but I could be wrong.

I was supposed to call this new client and tell him when I would arrive so he could meet me there, and we could palpate his horse to see if she was pregnant. But it turned out that he had an appointment and could not be there, which left me alone to catch and palpate a perfect stranger's horse. I didn't like it.

I came to a brick home with a large backyard. The horses were in the lot next to the house, and a row of eight-foot-tall sheds separated the two areas. The instructions called for me to pull into the alley and enter through the back gate.

I was told that there were stocks where I could put the mare to palpate her and a halter would be tied to the fence. Of course, I could not locate the stocks, and the only thing tied to the fence was a lead rope. To make matters worse, there was a round pen in the middle of the square lot next to the house, and four horses. Have you ever tried to catch one of four horses that are running around a circular object? It's pretty much impossible; they stayed on the other side of that round pen no matter what I did.

I went about building a barrier that would stop them. It took about fifteen minutes of Aggie ingenuity, but I managed it. I finally got them cornered and picked out the only mare in the bunch. She was a wild thing. I got the lead rope around her neck, only to find that she didn't like it at all. She reared and pitched a fit.

I was trying to calm her down, when a voice from the adjoining backyard came rising through the air: "Hello?"

The voice was a welcome melody at a trying moment. I began to talk back in a fervent tone.

"Yes, I'm Dr. Brock, and I'm here to palpate this mare. Could you please tell me where a halter might be?"

I was speaking in a tone somewhere between yelling and civil conversation. I meant to be polite yet convey a sense of aggravation over the unorganized state in which I found myself.

"Hello?" was all I got in response.

I started analyzing the voice to see if I could get an idea of who might be beckoning me. The tone sounded a bit like an older woman who could be staying at the house and wondering who was in the yard chasing the horses.

I changed my tone a bit to accommodate an older woman, which meant adding a bit more volume, along with more respect.

"Yes, I'm Dr. Brock, and I have come to see if this mare is pregnant. I was told there were some stocks around here that I could use to restrain her. Do you know where the rest of this halter is?"

My words were met with several minutes of silence. The pause led me to wonder just how old this woman might be. I pictured in my mind a gray-haired woman inching across the yard with a walker, trying to adjust her hearing aid to pick up the tones and wondering who was kicking up all this dust. I decided to raise my volume a little more and add more respect.

*"Yes, I'm Dr. Brock, and I was needing—"*

Before I could get any more words out, she interrupted with a remark that made me wonder if she might be getting a bit senile.

"Well, my stars!"

What did that mean? It seemed like a poor conversational placement for those words. My grandmothers always said words like that—things like "lands a Goshen" and "well, forevermore." They said phrases such as, "well, for Pete's sake" and "for the love of Pete." (Who the heck is Pete?) This further raised my suspicion that the speaker must be an old woman.

I decided to tie the horse to the fence and talk to this woman face-to-face in the backyard. But there was no one in the yard. No footprints in the dirt, no evidence of anyone with a walker. The back door was locked tight, and no one was visible through the back windows. Maybe I was dreaming. Was I losing my mind? Hearing things? Maybe someone was deliberately messing with me, but that would be a bad joke to play on a vet you'd never met before.

Just as I was about to make it to the end of the row of sheds and return to the lot full of horses, I heard the voice again: "Hello?"

Then I realized it was coming from a thicket of trees in the opposite corner. I made my way over and parted the vegetation.

There she was—a large, blue macaw parrot.

I'd just carried on a twenty-minute conversation with a bird. To make matters worse, it looked like the bird was laughing at me.

My next step was what any noble veterinarian would have done. I scanned the area to make sure no one had just seen me make an idiot of myself.

I finally found the stocks and managed to get the mare into them. She was pregnant.

Having done my job, I promptly got out of there before someone showed up and that bird told him how dumb the new veterinarian was.

☙❧

Mystery: A Mini-Epilogue

I could never do this story justice. When I figured out what had just happened, I laughed hysterically all by myself as I stood there and looked at that dang bird.

I rewrote this story four times trying to ooze the emotion I went through to anyone who might read it. I really don't think that I ever totally got it right. It is kinda like stepping off a curb, falling all the way to the ground, and then popping up and looking around to make sure no one saw. When you spend twenty minutes believing that you are talking to a person, only to find out it is a bird and you should have realized it, now that is a curb-falling moment that you hope no one witnessed.

# Moment 3

*Goose*

Sometimes I think *Crocodile Dundee* doesn't have a thing on veterinarians. We never know what the day holds, and sometimes it holds more than we expect.

The complaint was a down cow. She had gone down sometime in the night and couldn't get up. It is a common problem with cows, and it's one of the most common reasons I go on calls.

When I left the clinic, I figured it was just another down cow and I would be back in a short while. I had not been to this farm before, but I knew where it was. The owner informed me that he would not be there but described in detail where the cow was.

I arrived and found things just as he had described them. I went through a gate and approached a run-down barn with chicken-wire pens all around it. It was obvious that the place had not been well cared for in years. There were animals of all kinds. I saw goats, peacocks, and pigs just running around loose, horses, barking dogs, rabbits in cages, chickens of all sizes and breeds, a llama, sheep, and a few dairy cows.

The directions said to go through the barn, and the cow would be just past the next gate, beyond the water trough.

I made my way to the barn and came to an incredible realization. The manure in the barn had built up so much over the years that I actually had to stoop over to walk. There must have been ten feet of manure covering the floor of this barn. I squatted down and began the trek. I was carrying a few things that I thought I might need to work on the cow. The farther I went, the lower the clearing became. By the time I was in the middle of the barn, I was on my hands and knees to go under each rafter. Wow!

About halfway through, I heard a loud noise coming at me from my left side. It was a gurgled, hissing sound that was accompanied by the sound of flat feet hitting on moist ground. It was dark in that direction, so I could not focus on what it was. My mind was racing as I anticipated the creature entering the columns of light that penetrated from various openings in the barn.

Until you are on your hands and knees atop a ten-foot manure pile inside a dimly lit barn, you never realize how big a male goose is. In fact, as this monster came into focus, he appeared to be about five feet tall! This goose had teeth, and one big horn in the middle of his head, or at least it appeared this way from my vantage point.

I was looking at my supplies to determine what would be best to use as a weapon to defend myself. This goose was coming fast, and he meant business. He had a supporting cast of about six female geese forming at this flanks. The moment found me under an extended joist and unable to stand up. I reached into my bag and retrieved a plastic bottle of glucose. I gripped it tightly in my right hand and prepared for the worst. I was wondering how much of this goose was bluff and how much was really fight. The question was answered a second later.

He spread his wings just before he got to me and then gave me a mighty peck on the side of my head and the brim of my cap. The entire time, he was making a wicked hissing sound, while the female chorus spread out and honked endlessly from all directions.

The repeated pecks to my head area only served to change my initial fear to anger. It hurt just enough to make me mad. I didn't know what to do. I did not want to hurt him, but I didn't want to keep taking a head peckin,' either!

By now, they had backed me into a corner. The noise level was remarkable as they honked and hissed at the intruding doctor. Here I was, in a barn full of dookie, backed into a corner, being attacked by a gaggle of geese. I was unable to stand up, had nothing to defend myself with but a bottle of glucose, and was afraid of hurting them if I retaliated too harshly.

I decided to try the "get big and get loud" approach, hoping this would scare them off. I got as tall as the area allowed and screamed, "Get outta here, goose!" at the top of my lungs. It worked. They ran off toward the door, flapping and honking as they went.

They stayed just beyond the shadow of the door and looked at me. As long as I was still, they were quiet and stayed away. If I made a movement to gather my things or head toward the door, they would honk and run my way. This went on for a few minutes while I pondered a plan. Finally, I decided simply to get up and go to the cow. If they got in my way, I would just run over them. I made my way in the direction of the cow. This infuriated them. They ran and hissed at me with all they had. I just plowed through them like a fullback and made it to the side of the cow.

I began my usual treatment to help the cow. A curious dog ambled over to investigate the situation, only to be chased off by the giant goose with a horn. It was very apparent that this goose ruled the farm. The treatment included a bottle of fluid to be given intravenously at a slow rate. I had to sit on the side of this cow for thirty minutes and defend myself from an attack force of geese. They never left, and I never gave up.

By the time I returned to the clinic, I felt like I had boxed twelve rounds. I decided I would rather combat a mad dog than a herd of geese in a manure-filled barn.

*twelve*

## Critters

# Moment 1

*Reindeer Games*

The cast of characters in our tale: Dr. Zach Smith, leading man; Jo, faithful technician; Berenda, faithful secretary; Kyle, Berenda's faithful husband; Manda, another faithful technician; Dr. Bo Brock, old man; Kerri, wife of the old man.

After so many years of working together, voice tone and inflections are sometimes more meaningful than words.

One afternoon, Jo, one of our technicians, came around the corner to ask for assistance. I didn't understand what she said, but I knew something was making her lips move faster than the words could come out. This is usually accompanied by her buns getting close to the ground as she prepares to spring into action.

Anytime Jo does this, there is an emergency.

I trotted out the back door to see the critter standing in the grass just north of the barn. No problem. We would just hem him up in the corner of the fence and the barn, and this emergency would be past tense. Wrong!

A reindeer has more moves than Barry Sanders does, and this one was glad to be free.

Dr. Zach Smith saw the developing situation and headed to saddle a horse.

Berenda, our secretary, saw the situation and headed in to call for help.

Kyle, Berenda's husband, saw the situation and headed for his pickup.

I saw the situation and visualized $5,000 worth of hundred-pound reindeer darting off toward the south at about forty miles per hour.

I took off on foot behind the rascal, just hoping to keep him in sight. The reindeer made a fast cut west and was heading straight for a set of corrals just south of the clinic. Manda, another technician, had anticipated well and was coming in from the flank to shut any gates and bring this chase to a quick end.

Just our luck. There was no place with a gate; only another corner. We slowed down this time and began creeping in. Just about the time we were closing in on the reindeer, the cavalry (Zach) mounted the hills.

It was at this point that the chase really began.

Berenda was busy calling people to help. She had cowboys and police saddling horses and devising strategies. Kerri drove up just as Zach headed down the road, hot on Rudolph's trail. As I opened the gate to let Zach into the pasture, I felt a bit of hope that he could rope that rascal, and this chase would be over. Zach is good with a rope, and now we had a wide-open space.

The deer stopped for a second, thinking that he would blend in with the cattle. Zach was hot on the trail. He picked that critter out and zoomed in like ugly on an ape. My anticipation mounted as I watched Zach (alias Roy Cooper) start swinging his rope. He was in perfect position for the catch when I saw the deer causally look over his shoulder. It was at this point that I realized that reindeer have a gear that horses don't have.

The deer headed east toward Los Ybanez, the local beer store. He had managed to lose everyone but Kerri in the Durango. When I caught up to them in my pickup, the deer was headed toward the prison. By now, the others had arrived. I was wondering what those prison guards were going to think when a reindeer followed by four vehicles and a horse came racing toward the gate.

At first I thought, *Great. That rascal won't be able to get out of that place.* But then it dawned on me. *I'm not sure if they are going to believe that a reindeer was running through a cotton field in West Texas. They may just shoot first and ask questions later.*

Thank goodness, we will never know because the speedy rascal turned north and headed for the airport. By now, the horse was out of the picture. He was run-down, and so was Zach. I handed the doctor my mobile phone and headed off to prevent a plane crash.

At the south end of the runway, Rudolph headed back to town. I couldn't decide if this was good or bad. It may be good because we could find a place to trap him; it may be bad because there was traffic. Traffic! Now I was thinking not only of a $5,000 reindeer, but also of a $30,000 car! This was turning into an expensive daydream.

Into town we sped. Kerri got lost somewhere in the chase, so this left three pickups and five people to keep the marathon-running deer from harm's way.

By now, this deer had run for about forty-five minutes and covered fifteen or so miles. He was starting to tire a little, but he looked like he was nowhere near spent. We came in on the east side of town. It was something else to observe the looks on people's faces as we raced from yard to yard, trying to corner a reindeer.

We would get him in a tight spot and then all jump out with ropes and nets. He would put a move on us, and then we would all run back to the trucks and tear out after him. This happened time and time again.

Finally, the deer darted between a house and a storage shed. I jumped out of the pickup and was first on the scene. There was a moment, as I approached him in this backyard, that time stopped, and we gazed into one another's eyes. By now, my adrenaline was at nearly toxic levels. Rudolph was looking a bit tired. But one thing was apparent: this was where the chase would end for one of us. He was getting out of this yard over my dead body.

He tried one of those halfback moves. *Not this time, buddy.* I got his left back leg as he bounced by. He was dragging me on my back across the yard, but I was not going to let go. That critter could have dragged me to Tahoka, but I was not lettin' go! About that time, Kyle rounded the corner and finished the capture.

Just think. An hour and a half earlier, I was back at the clinic thinking this would be no big deal.

Berenda managed to call off the posse. We got Rudolph back to the clinic in one piece. He was panting a bit, but seemed none the worse for wear. No wonder Santa chose these beasts to pull a sleigh all over the world in one night!

# Moment 2

### Skunks

"I told Papa not to throw them scraps off the back porch," a voice whined on the other end of the phone.

It was Mrs. Olgien, and the voice reflected her remorse for having to call me on Christmas Eve combined with her anger at Papa for being too lazy to walk out to the chicken yard. I had never met them or been to their house. My first Christmas as a veterinarian might as well have taken me on another adventure.

Cold was an understatement for the effects that a twenty-five-mile-per-hour north wind had on the rolling canyons of Clarendon, Texas. I was dreading leaving the warmth of the house for such a petty call. It seemed that the combination of scraps and warmth under the Olgiens' house had lured a skunk. Somehow this critter had wedged himself between two footers under the house and was very stuck. The family had discovered the culprit before he could empty his stink bomb. My assignment was to sedate the skunk without releasing the bomb and then carefully remove him from the premises. I was still new in the community and very much wanted to please these people and perhaps make some new friends.

As I arrived at the scene, the reasons for living in extremely rural America came flooding into my thoughts.

I was twenty miles from the closest anywhere, and there must have been ten cars around this house. A combination of family in for Christmas and neighbors had made this home the hot place for Christmas Eve. One of the cars in the yard had the insignia of the Donley County Sheriff's Department, indicating that even the law would be involved.

All of the parking spots close to the house were already taken. This gave me about a hundred-yard walk to the house to focus on my mission and be thankful that the house faced north and the skunk was under the back porch.

As I rounded the line of prairie-planted windbreak trees, I noticed the lights were on in the living room, which was just inside the holiday-light-surrounded glass front door. The womenfolk were gathered in this front room, while none of the men was in sight.

"You better get in here, Dr. Bo," the much-toned-down voice of Mrs. Olgien greeted me. "The men are in the backyard trying to figure out how to get the varmint."

I was quickly introduced to everyone in the room and then escorted to the back.

About fifteen men stood in the backyard, sizing me up as I exited the house with Mamma. After a thorough briefing, I scooted under the porch to a two-foot-square opening that led to the substructure of the house. Upon peering through, I caught my first glimpse of the skunk's fanny. It was not at all as I had pictured the situation. The skunk was wedged between two boards and was about seven feet away. There was no way I could get a shot of sedative into one of those buns and then get away before the explosion of stink.

I backed out, and we brainstormed. Finally, we decided to tape a syringe to the end of a broom and use a very small needle to deliver the drug. The small needle might just be gentle enough to keep the skunk from spraying, but just in case, I would be a long way off.

I filled the syringe with about twice the dose of sedative that I would have given a cat. I felt like G. I. Joe as I belly crawled, inch by inch, toward the trespasser. Carefully glancing around the protection of the footer, I gently inserted the tiny needle into the left bun of the skunk and slipped him a Mickey. Not a drop of odor entered the air. What an accomplishment! I scurried out to a hero's welcome. I felt sure I would be on *Wild Kingdom* after such an adventure-filled mission.

We went back into the house and enjoyed the fruits of our labor, a cup of Mamma's hot chocolate, as we waited for the sedative to take effect. We visited and laughed for a few minutes, and then I started my hero's departure.

I was about to leave when Mamma asked if we had actually removed the now-snoring skunk. "No," was my answer, but I assured her that it would just take a second, and I would do it before I left.

A few of the men went out with me as I crawled back under the house to retrieve the sleeping skunk.

I peered in at the now-limp tail of the skunk and quickly closed the seven-foot gap that separated us. The thing was stuck harder than I had figured. I pulled and tugged with little success. By now, thirty minutes had passed since the shot. When the skunk finally came sliding free, our eyes met. It was at this moment that I realized that the drug had worn off.

This critter had been chased by dogs, wedged between boards, injected with a needle, and had never released a drop of liquid stink. But the minute our eyes met, he fogged up the world. He got me right on the side of the head. Under the house is no place to jump back; if you do, you will bump your head, and that's exactly what I did.

Only the toughest of the bunch were still in the yard. They knew before I backed out that the mission had taken a serious turn.

I could hear the sheriff saying something about clearing the area and forming a perimeter. My eyes were watering so much that I couldn't see a thing. This was nothing like the smell you get when you pass a dead skunk in the road. The smell stinks, but this smell actually hurts. There were parts of my body other than my nose that were smelling this. It was then that I felt something warm and liquid running down my neck.

Did I mention that I can't stand to see my own blood? That's right. I can do a C-section on a cow while eating a hamburger, but a steady flow of my own blood, and I am going to pass out. Maybe it means I'm a sissy, but I have no control over it. I can take kicks, cuts, and contusions just fine, but bleeding takes me down.

My knuckles were white from the tight grip I had on Mr. Skunk. I never let go as I backed out from under the porch. Here I stood, surrounded by a ring of people I had never met, holding a skunk on Christmas Eve, about to pass out.

Everyone backed off even farther as the smell engulfed the area. I heard someone say, "He's bleeding all over the place."

The next few scenes happened in slow motion for me. First I dropped to my knees and then to my stomach. That was the last thing I remember until I came to in the garage with Mamma rubbing my head with a cold rag.

I stank. The four men who had carried me to the garage stank, the women who had taken off my coat and boots stank, and my pickup stank for two months just from carrying me home.

They would have been better off if they had never met me. I took two baths in tomato juice but still had to sleep on a towel-covered couch for three days.

I talked to Mrs. Olgien a week or so later, and she told me that it still smelled in the house but that they had gotten used to it. The moral of the story: don't visit too long on Christmas Eve after shooting a skunk with twice the cat dose of sedative. Merry Christmas, everyone.

# Moment 3

*Snakes*

G rowing up in the countryside of West Texas, I spent most of my time outdoors, where I had the opportunity to see, catch, and torment every kind of critter this part of the world has to offer.

One day, however, I was surprised to see a portion of a coiled snake that looked like no snake I had ever seen. It was inside a cardboard box in the storage house I was cleaning. The visible portion was gray, and the scales appeared large and rough. I am not afraid of snakes. If they rattle, I stay away; if they don't, they usually just slither away.

I simply picked up the box, carried it outside, and dropped it on the ground, assuming the snake would take off, and I could then finish sorting the things in the box.

Not the case.

The snake stayed put.

I thought it might have crawled into the box and died, but I wasn't about to reach inside to find out. Instead, I picked up a pig-show stick and decided to poke the thing a few times to get it on the move.

The box was now on its side. In the outdoor light, the body portion I could see was fairly thick, and the skin still had that unfamiliar gray gleam.

What happened next took only about five seconds, but seemed like one of those slow-motion segments in an action movie: I poked the snake with the stick, and it came out of that box like a bolt of lightning. It must have been seven feet long and seemed like the most evil creature I'd ever encountered.

It moved so fast I could barely get a good look until it raised its head about three feet off the ground and started right toward me. It began hissing and spitting and was moving so fast I had no time to contemplate what to do next.

So I did what my fight-or-flight mechanism dictated: I started swinging that show stick like a hyperactive Zorro in a swordfight and screaming like a little girl.

What was this thing? I was quickly backing up while swinging the stick as fast as I could.

I backed onto the step of the storage shed and could feel myself going down. Oh no, this would bring me down to eye level with the creature, and, even worse, I'd have to stop swinging the stick to catch myself.

About the time my fanny hit the ground, however, the snake turned and sped off faster than a dog can run. It disappeared into the bushes and left me sitting there with a speeding pulse.

I wondered what it could be. The more I thought about it, the more it reminded me of a black mamba we had seen at a zoo a few years before. But what was a black mamba doing in Lamesa? Those things live in Africa.

I was beginning to wonder if someone was mad at me because his horse didn't live and had released a mamba at our house. I went inside and told the kids not to venture outside for a while. I wondered how I might contact Jack Hanna, because I couldn't think of anyone else who could handle a mamba.

I told Kerri, "I'm afraid the dogs may be dead in the morning. I think I just saw a black mamba in the storage shed, and it is the deadliest snake in the world."

"You're crazy," she replied and went on about her business.

The next day, when I told some people at church about the snake, they laughed and told me it was simply a coachwhip. I had never seen one in my entire life, but after researching it on the Internet, I believe they were right. I am still amazed at how fast that snake could move.

If you ever see a gray-looking snake with large, rough scales, run away. It may not be deadly, but it will scare you half to death.

# *Section 4*

## Clients

The primary function of money is an expression of character, and only the second as a means of exchange.

Collin, the Grandfather
2012

*thirteen*

## Old People

# Old People

Perspective is what makes us who we are. The way we process the information that is presented to us and react to it determines the way the rest of the world perceives us. This precept fascinates me. Being a practicing veterinarian in a small town demands that I understand this concept.

Doing the same thing over and over and expecting a different outcome is perhaps the definition of ignorance. I have spent my life doing that and certainly continue to do it even though I know that it is ignorant. I suppose old people have just had more time to do the same things over and over. It appears to me, that this repetition of life events results in a perspective that we call wisdom.

I guess it just happens that when a person repeats the same situations that life offers, a predictable outcome usually occurs, and old people have that concept down. They may not verbalize it or even have it grouped into an organized thought, but they know it.

It is this view of life that comes from experience that makes me love to watch older people live. My mother has entered that time in her life. She is seventy-four years old now and has endured all that life has offered, and somehow she maintains a personality that makes everyone around her smile.

She is the last living person in my life from the big six—that is, my parents and both sets of grandparents. These are the people who give us our genetic view of the world and the ones whose reactions we watch as we encounter life. The fact that she is the last one left has given me an uninterrupted view of the way she sees things.

As I observed my mother this weekend as we all set around the living room and doted on Lilli, our first grandchild and her first great-grandchild, I mused about how much of my world perspective I picked up from her. She has analyzed life for twenty-four years longer than I have, and it would do me good to try to understand how she sees the world now. I did this, without her even knowing it, by asking her questions about life in the middle of normal conversations. She would go off answering and filling my brain with her genetics and making everyone in the room laugh and smile.

This is the perspective that I am lucky she gave me. She can hold the serious and tragic situations that life offers within her and use them for the wisdom that it takes to carry on. Yet somehow, she has learned that tragedy and seriousness are best replaced by "happy." Yes, this is what she does; she looks for the smile in a puddle of mud, the laughter in gloomy air, and the wisdom of not taking herself or life too seriously.

Old people are funny; they have an appreciation for things that younger people often can't yet understand.

# Moment 1

*Old Men*

*Tall Cow, Fat*

The trailer rolled into the parking lot of the clinic, eliciting sighs of awe and amazement from the group of onlookers. Mr. Pep was his name, and he was bringing in his sick cow. The other clients who happened to be at the clinic with me stood with dropped jaws as he pulled across the expanse from the road to the building.

It's not every day you see a cow riding on a flatbed trailer. This was no ordinary flatbed; it must have been five feet off the ground, and it had a cow strapped down on it with those "come along"-type straps that people use to bind round bales—not your ordinary bovine-delivery method.

Ol' Pep had called early that morning to tell me that he had a "real sick" cow that I needed to come out and examine. My reply included phrases such as, "I'm really busy this morning. It will be quite a while before I can get away. It would be better if you could bring her in. I don't want anything to happen to her, so we could get to her quicker if you could load her up." And, "Get her here as quick as you can."

It was 5:00 p.m. now, and I had almost completely forgotten he had phoned.

Strapped to that five-foot-high trailer was the skinniest cow I had ever seen. She looked like something from an Ace Reid cartoon. Every rib was visible, and her flanks almost touched in the middle. I was amazed.

"What are you feeding her, Pep?" was all I could think to say as I stood above her.

"I got a giant pile of food for 'em out there," he replied with great conviction.

"Do all of your cows look like this?" was the next logical question.

"No, about half of 'em are big and fat."

The last thing you ever want to do is argue with a convinced cow raiser about nutrition; I learned that early on in my veterinary career. So, I treated the cow the best I could, and Pep went merrily on his way.

Three days later, he called me to come out to treat another cow that had gone down. This time, things around the clinic were not so hectic, and I drove out to his place on the outskirts of Clarendon. He had told me that the cow we treated at the clinic was much better, but now another one was down, and two or three of the others were in bad shape. What I saw when I arrived amazed me. This guy must have had a hundred cows grazing in what looked like a junkyard. There was junk scattered everywhere.

I stood in the middle of this "pasture" and looked at the scattered herd. He was right; some of the cows were big and fat, but others were as poor as any cattle I had seen in my life. My mind was racing with all the differential diagnoses they had filled my brain with in vet school. I was thinking about disease, poisoning, bad teeth in the old cows, and other things that had big, Latin-sounding words.

As I pondered the situation with puzzlement and perplexity, something suddenly hit me: all the fat cows were tall, and all the short cows were skinny. My eyes moved from cow to cow...tall cow, fat...short cow, skinny...tall cow, fat...short cow, skinny. It went on and on and the pattern held with no variance as I looked over the entire herd.

"Pep, where is this pile of food you told me about?"

"Over there behind the barn."

"You mind if I have a look at it?"

"Shoot no, come on over."

As we rounded the corner, the answer became apparent. There, about ten feet behind the barn, sat another flatbed trailer that was five feet off the ground. Surrounding it was a large group of short cattle that were straining their necks, trying to get to the "pile" of food that the tall cows had eaten back.

I counseled with Pep for a while about pushing that feed off the trailer so the short cows could get to it. I could tell he thought that was going to be too much work, but he grudgingly agreed that he would do something to remedy the situation.

I was driving by Mr. Pep's place about a month later and decided to stop by and see how the short cows were faring. He was nowhere to be found, so I drove on over to the pasture and began analyzing the cows. Things were looking good—tall cow, fat...short cow, fat.

I went around behind the barn to see how the problem had been addressed, and you will never believe what I found. There, in the same place it had been before, was the flatbed trailer with a pile of food on it. The only difference was that he had hired a backhoe to dig a pit into which he could drive that trailer. Now the trailer was lower to the ground, and all the cattle could get to the pile.

They just can't teach stuff like this in vet school.

# Moment 2

*Screw Down*

"**W**here is that young veterinarian? I need to have a word with him! He gave my horse a shot of screw-down medicine, and I didn't know it!"

I was in the other room, but I recognized the voice. It was Skeet Black. He was a seventy-eight-year-old ranch foreman, who had retired about five months earlier after having been foreman on the same ranch for fifty years. And I knew that the young veterinarian he was speaking of was me.

I had been a veterinarian for only about three months, and things weren't coming too easy. Seemed like I would have weeks when everything I tried to do just went wrong. I was living through one of those weeks when Skeet's very distinctive old cowboy voice came floating in from the waiting room to the small-animal surgery room where I was spaying a dog.

The dog spay wasn't going very well. It was a four-year-old, in-heat Labrador, and I was beginning to think I would rather have jock itch myself than spay fat dogs. Everything that could possibly go wrong in a spay was going wrong, and now I had to shift my focus to an old cowboy dude who was obviously mad at me about something. I hadn't even seen this guy for a month. What could I have done to his horse that took an entire month to finally go wrong, and why did he have to come in hollering at the very moment when my horrible surgery skills were captivating my attention?

Screw-down medicine? What in the heck was that? I had been outta school only a few months, but I'd had about 350 hours of college, and I had never heard that term even once.

Let me see, what had I done to his mare? Oh yeah, Skeet had retired and decided to take up team roping. He bought a twenty-two-year-old mare that was a seasoned head horse, and he was roping with some of the locals. He had brought her in because she was not coming out of the box fast enough and wasn't turning quick enough to face. I remembered it well now.

My attention momentarily switched back to the bleeding fat Lab. I was so frustrated with spaying fat dogs that I quit considering Skeet for a moment, until his next words penetrated the surgery room.

"You say he is doing a surgery? Well, I am just gonna wait right here till he gets done. I need to have a word with that fella, and I am not gonna leave until I do."

His voice rang with aggravation and bordered on mad. Apparently, I had given this screw-down medicine to his mare, and something about it had ticked off this old rascal. I was scanning my burdened brain for what I had done to this horse. All I did was inject her hock joints with some triamcinolone. She had bone spavin in those hocks, and I just wanted to give her old joints some relief so she could carry this seventy-eight-year-old fart up and down a roping arena without any pain. I figured this would make her go faster and feel better, and everyone would be happy. I had done it on horses before, and everyone seemed to like it...but not ol' Skeet.

I finally was finishing up the wretched spay and knew I would have to face him shortly. I had no idea what he was gonna say or why I was in trouble. My stomach was in knots, almost like when I would get sent to the principal's office in the fifth grade for doing something for which elementary-school turdheads needed a swat or two.

Get a picture of what I was about to face in your mind. Just outside the door stood a man who was a ranch foreman for fifty years. When he brought the mare in, this guy stood in front of me, rolled his own cigarette, and smoked it. He had ridden horses for so long that his forty-or-so-inch–inseam Levi's 501s had a permanent bow in them. He wore long-sleeved shirts with those snap buttons when they were completely out of style. His cowboy hat was so ancient and weathered that the brim had taken on the shape of a taco, and the sweat ring extended up to the crown. His boots came to a point, and the leather was so worn that it was as thin as the skin on his giant earlobes. And this fella sounded as if he was furious with me.

I finally worked up the courage to open the door to the surgery room and face ol' Skeet. I was still shaking with aggravation from the terrible time I had just had spaying the dog. When I opened the door, I couldn't believe what I saw.

There stood cowboy Skeet in a pair of Nike sweatpants and house shoes. He was leaning over a walker that was seven inches too short for his long, lanky frame, and he didn't have his false teeth in, which made him look ninety-five instead of seventy-eight.

"There you are, you young veterinary rascal," he said as he saw my figure appear in the slowly opening door.

"Let me tell you som'in', youngun. I don't know what it was that you gave my mare, but it made her feel so good that she left me in the box when she took off. You told me to stay off her for three days and then start roping again. Well, I did, and that critter took off so fast that I just flew over the cantle of that saddle, bounced off her butt, and landed straddle of the fence that goes around Lester's roping arena. Doctor said I was lucky to have any balls left after that spill. Now I gotta hip that is aching and have to walk along behind this walker thing for a month.

"I just come in to tell you that you better tell people to 'screw down' after you give one of them there shots. I am tellin' ya, that critter can run fast and fart loud. Now don't you forget it!"

I have done just what he told me. That conversation took place nearly twenty-five years ago, and if you ever come to the clinic with a horse that needs its hock injected, don't be surprised if I tell you, "Now, when I give this, you better screw down, 'cause this rascal is gonna run fast and fart loud!"

# Moment 3

*Tex*

We had three horses with serious colic, a pig under anesthesia, a cow with a prolapse that was trying to have a baby, and a waiting room full of dogs. It is times like these that you can't decide what to do first, and everyone needs you right now. But none of them needed us more than Tex did.

Tex was standing patiently with his horse while he waited his turn. The horse was very sick, and it appeared as if we were going to have to do a colic surgery. The anesthetized pig was on the surgery table with its nose covered by an oxygen mask, and the cow was in the chute, straining and grunting to no avail.

I had gone into the clinic to get instruments to do the pig surgery, when my ear caught that spine-tingling sound of someone gagging as though he might throw up. With all the nasty smells that a veterinary clinic can produce, this sound happens on occasion. I looked back out the door into the large-animal part of the clinic just in time to see ol' Tex go down.

I thought this to be a bit strange; the guy just piled up in the corner in a position that any normal fifty-five-year-old had avoided for at least forty-five years. It was as if he was sitting down, but both of his feet were higher than his head. This caused me some stress.

Dr. Zach Smith was looking at me while I looked out the door. He had heard the retching, but he couldn't see through the doorway. He must have detected the panic on my face, because we both ran for the door at the same time.

Tex was trying to get his feet from behind his head when we approached. I wasn't sure what had happened, but I knew it was going to take some doing to get him out of the knot he had fallen into. Zach pulled one way, and I pulled the other. With a few tugs, Tex uncoiled and stood.

"I just gotta get a little air," he managed as he headed for the garage door.

We followed him with great concern as he bent over the tailgate of the pickup. I was a bit worried, and the expression on Zach's face was no consolation, either.

"You gonna be all right?" Zach asked.

"Just need a little air is all," Tex muttered.

"Why don't we take you inside and let you lay on the couch for a minute?" Zach persisted.

To my surprise, Tex agreed.

You know when a tough ol' cowboy dude says he'll go inside and lie down, something is terribly wrong. Zach and I each took a side; about three steps into the journey, Tex collapsed. Zach caught him, and we carried him over to the horse-surgery table.

Now we had a pig anesthetized on the pig-surgery table, Tex's horse rolling around in pain on the floor of the surgery room, Tex passed out on the horse-surgery table not two feet from the sleeping pig, and neither of us knew what to do next.

I remember thinking that Tex would be given pretty good care if he were a pig or a horse. Zach didn't look too confident, either. We went to work anyway.

Zach was feeling for a pulse in his wrist, and I was listening to his chest with a stethoscope. Neither of us found a thing.

"Oh my, oh my, oh my," I stammered as I grabbed the pulse oximeter off the pig's tongue and hooked it to Tex. It read a heart rate of 180 and a blood-oxygen count of seventy-six; you need ninety-five.

Zach stayed fairly composed, but I panicked. I grabbed the oxygen mask off the pig and put it on Tex. I started moving toward the chest; I figured if there was any CPR fixin' to happen, Zach could have the mouth-to-mouth part, and I would do the chest compressions. We met at the chest.

"You'd better call the ambulance, Bo," Zach lamented.

I'd be willing to wager that it was the first time an ambulance driver rolled onto a scene where two veterinarians were treating a sick cowboy like a pig having a heart attack. We had him hooked to monitors, and we were giving him oxygen through the pig mask. We were listening to his chest and trying to check eye responses.

In our combined fifteen years of veterinary experience, we had treated at least a hundred crashing animals, but we were overwhelmed with the prospect of losing one human life.

Everything turned out OK. Tex went to the Lamesa Hospital, where they fixed him up and had him back at the clinic in about four hours. His ticker was fine; he was hypoglycemic. I talked to him the other day, and he said the only side effects from the entire ordeal are a faint oink when he coughs and a subconscious urge to root around in the dirt of the backyard.

# Moment 4

### *The Old Man and the Open Cows*

I can remember looking down and seeing "8:02" on the digital clock in the pickup as I pulled up to the ranch.

I use the term "ranch" loosely because this gentleman had only seventeen cows. We had a busy morning scheduled, and with any luck, I would be back to the clinic by nine o'clock and could start getting caught up. After all, how long could it take to palpate seventeen cows for pregnancy? At some of the ranches my associate and I go to, we can palpate 750 to 800 head in a day.

I had never met this fellow but I was not surprised to see that he was old. His voice on the phone sounded like each breath could have been his last. I watched him mosey out of the front door of a stucco house that had not been painted or repaired in any way for what looked like about fifty years. He must have been about six foot five inches and weighed about 125 pounds. He was so thin and wore such tight jeans that it looked as if his legs bent four or five times before they connected with his feet. He was wearing one of those Western shirts with snaps for buttons and had a giant bandana tied around his neck. His boots were straight out of a grade-B Western movie. They were so pointed that his toes just had to be setting one atop the other in order to conform to the shape they were forced to comply with.

The only piece of attire that did not fit the Western motif was his hat. The hat looked like the one that the engineer on *Petticoat Junction* wore. It was made out of striped mattress ticking material and had been worn so much that it had taken on a lean to the left side of his head.

He never spoke a word as he approached. He just pointed over to a set of run-down sheds and a working pen about the size of a football field.

I put the pickup back in drive and headed over. He ambled across the yard at a snail's pace and began to talk long before I could hear what he was saying.

I began to size up the situation. Seventeen cows of various sizes and shapes stood in the middle of a one-acre trap. In the center of the trap was the oldest squeeze chute I had ever seen. There were no alleys leading to the chute at all. It just sat alone like a centerpiece on a Thanksgiving table. In fact, there was no fence in the entire trap, except the one that made up the perimeter.

It was obvious that he had coaxed the cattle in from a large pasture that was out the south end of the trap. These cows did not look like they had been handled much. They were looking at me with wide nostrils and high heads.

He was still mumbling as he approached, but I was not concerned with what he was saying. I was concentrating on the logistics of an eighty-year-old man and a thirty-five-year-old veterinarian getting seventeen snorting cows through a squeeze chute with no alleys leading to it. I was beginning to think that this was going to put me a little behind on the tidy schedule the secretary had booked for the day.

When his ramblings finally penetrated the my wall of thoughts, I was contemplating, it became apparent that one of the cows might be a little dangerous. He called the red one "a bit snakey." Having been around old cowboy dudes all my life, I knew what this meant: look out! He was not kidding, either. The rascal would leave the pack and charge anything that came into the pen.

Here is the situation: Grandpa and I were going to carry twenty pipe panels that probably weigh about 300 pounds each from a barn a hundred yards away to construct an alley leading to an antique chute, all while ducking a "snakey" red cow. This guy took a full five minutes to walk across the yard. It was becoming clear that I was going to be more than a little behind when I got back to the clinic.

The red, glowing letters on the dash of the pickup said 10:29 as I plopped into the seat for a drink of water. Just two and a half hours were required to "throw up a few panels." My back was aching, and my patience totally gone.

The red cow liked the old man. It was me she wanted to charge. She would run back and forth around him, and he would never even change expressions. She must have blown two gallons of snot on me, and I must have kicked two tons of dirt on her. If those panels weighed 300 pounds apiece, I was carrying 285 pounds, and he was carrying fifteen. But that was not the bad part. Because he walked so slowly, I had to carry 285 pounds about five times longer than I would have if I had pulled each one of them over by myself. Oh, but he insisted on helping.

The clock in the pickup read 12:02 as I sat in the front seat wondering why not one cow was pregnant. He had "run" up to the house to get some paperwork, while I wondered how I was going to salvage the rest of the day. By now, most of the early appointments had probably left, and the later ones were pacing the floor and calling me names.

My right index finger had been mashed in the mechanical squeeze chute. You see, I would push the cattle up, catch the head, squeeze her, open the tailgate, put a pipe behind each one, palpate her, mark on her with a paint stick, and finally let her go. His contribution to the entire process was to give me a verbal history of every cow.

When he finally returned, I told him that since every cow was open, we really needed to test his bull.

To this he replied, "What bull? I ain't got no bull. Haven't had one in over a year!"

I could feel my blood pressure going up. What in the world was this guy thinking? I spent all morning palpating cows that he said should have been having calves three months ago, only to find out that he doesn't even have a bull. I was about to explode with some "anger-inspired" statements, when he interrupted me with a quote that I will never forget: "I don't need no bull. Been feedin' 'em them there breeder's cubes for about a year now."

*Oh my*, was my recurring theme as I drove home. *Three dollars a head*, crossed my mind a few times as I cruised along. That's right. Fifty-one bucks plus a small call fee was what I had to show for my morning's effort. It had crossed my mind as we constructed the working pens that none of those cows looked pregnant. It had crossed my mind a few times that there was no bull. It had crossed my mind a few times that I should have been getting a history while we worked. But it never crossed my mind that anyone would ever think that "breeder's cubes" would make a cow pregnant.

# Moment 5

## The Old Man and the Tree

It was about closing time, and I was thinking how nice it would be to leave on time for a change, when the phone rang.

The man on the other end of the line sounded like the oldest living human.

He was trying to explain how his prize heifer was down having a baby, but he could barely complete a sentence before starting a different subject.

It was apparent that there was no way he could bring the cow in because it couldn't stand up, so I packed all the stuff I thought might be needed and headed off with the worst set of directions imaginable.

By the time I arrived at the "ranch," it was pitch-dark and colder than a frog.

I saw the old man standing next to a sky-blue 1977 pickup truck with a scrap-iron headache rack on it and one of those old coiled CB antennas still attached to the rack. He didn't even move when we left our vehicle and walked over to him. He was leaning against the pickup, his eyes closed. I stood right in front of him and finally came to the conclusion that he was asleep. That's right; he had dozed off while standing.

I spoke a few words at a moderate volume. Nothing. I raised my voice a bit, and this brought him back to the world.

"I am Dr. Brock, and I have come to deliver your calf," poured from my mouth with that I-am-talking-to-an-old-man volume and tone.

This only made him bring a cupped hand to his ear and utter a hearty, "Huh?"

I repeated myself at near-screaming level.

"Oh, it's not my heifer; it's Daddy's," he said.

Did I hear correctly? This guy still has a living father who owns cattle?

About that time, the passenger door of the pickup opened, and "Daddy" slid out. He was bent into a permanent comma, with about fifty gray hairs growing from a spot in the middle of his head, and no teeth. He was wearing overalls and no coat.

Then the driver's door opened, and the brother of Ol' Sleepy got out.

None of them could hear. They all talked at the same time. I gathered from the chatter that the cow was out in the pasture and that they wanted me to get my stuff and ride in the back of their truck. So I did.

My technician, Manda, came along. I asked her to follow us outside the fence, and said I would call her on the cell phone if we needed anything.

We drove into the darkness for what seemed like an hour and finally found the heifer. She was on her side with just the head of the calf sticking out. I jumped out with a rope to tie her so we could pull the calf, but the second she saw me, she jumped up and ran off.

Picture the situation: I am in the middle of a five-square-mile pasture with three guys who are clinically deaf, trying to catch a wild heifer and deliver a calf. Furthermore, it seems I am going to have to rope the critter from the back of a '77 sky-blue pickup with Daddy at the controls.

Off we went. The heifer was heading for a draw with a thick stand of salt cedars in it, so I really needed to get the rope on her fast. Daddy must have noticed this about the same time, because he gunned the truck and brought me in perfect position to toss my loop. Surprisingly, I caught her on the first throw.

Now what? There was nothing to attach the rope to except that wire-loop CB antenna. It was well anchored to the headache rack, so much so that when the cow hit the end of the rope, the antenna held firm. Unfortunately, the headache rack didn't. It flew out of the truck bed as the heifer kept running, dragging my rope, the CB antenna, and the headache rack, with the old man hot on her trail.

As luck would have it, she got the entire contraption lodged in the first tree she passed. This stopped her and gave me time to jump out. I'm not sure what I thought I was going to do with a thousand-pound cow on the end of a rope hung up in a four-foot cedar sapling, but jumping out seemed like the thing to do.

When she saw me, she started running around the tree, and this caused Daddy, for some reason, to start chasing her around the tree in the truck.

"Stop chasing her," I yelled, waving my arms.

He heard nothing, and just kept driving around the sapling in smaller and smaller circles until he finally went right over the top of it. The front of the truck made it over the tree, but when the back end was directly on top of it, it lifted the rear of the truck right off the ground.

The fact that he'd stopped moving made the old man press harder on the gas pedal, spinning the tires a million miles an hour. The engine screamed like a jet, but he had no idea what was going on.

I was standing in front of the truck thinking that, if that little tree broke, I would surely die. I jumped out of the way just in time to hear it snap and see that sky-blue pickup take off like a jet from a carrier.

In less than a second, the truck disappeared into the cedar thicket, but then the motor died, and things got very quiet. I heard the doors open, and in a few minutes, they all meandered out.

The cow was gone.

I called Manda to come and get us. We drove back to their house listening to them all talk at once about the adventure. I called them several times the next day but never got an answer.

As far as I know, that truck is still in the cedars, and my rope is still attached to the cow.

# Moment 6

### U-Haul

It was a thirty-mile journey from Memphis, Texas, to Clarendon, Texas, a nice four-lane highway all the way. I had made the trip many times when I practiced in the booming metropolis of Clarendon.

I was the only veterinarian at the clinic on this day, and things were busy. Boog Peacock was the man's name, and he had a "cut-up" horse. His voice was frantic and riddled with worried tones. The horse had gotten into the fence and laccrated its front leg in several places. Ol' Boog wanted me to leave right then and drive to Memphis to suture this horse back together. The problem was, I was snowed under; I could not just up and leave. It was a choice you often have to make as a veterinarian. Do you want to make one person mad, or do you want to make eight or nine people—who are already at the clinic or on their way—mad?

I told Boog to bring the horse in. He said he couldn't because he had no trailer. I told him to borrow one. He said none of his friends had horses or cows. I told him he was just going to have to figure something out because it would be hours before I could make it.

The morning had turned into afternoon, and I had forgotten about Boog. When you are a recent graduate, each case takes all of your concentration. It was about four o'clock when some elderly cowboy showed up at the clinic with a horse. He had come from Memphis and was going on with another client about the strange sight he had seen on the trip to Clarendon. I was only half paying attention when I looked across the parking lot and saw the sight with my own eyes.

Some things are just too amazing for words. My mouth fell open, and I just watched as Boog pulled into the drive to the clinic. He had

163

the horse. He had made the thirty miles from Memphis on the four-lane highway. He was ready to have the horse sewed up. But I remained flabbergasted.

I stood there and wondered what I would have done if my horse was cut up and I had no trailer. I thought of dozens of possibilities, but I never would have thought of doing what he had done. Coming across the parking lot was a blue, 1975 pickup truck with a trailer behind it. It was no ordinary trailer. It was a flatbed U-Haul trailer with a horse on it. The horse was tied to the front of the trailer with what looked like about six feet of binder twine.

Let me describe the way the horse looked. It was standing with its legs spread as far apart as a horse can manage. His eyes were wide open, and his eyebrows were rounded, giving him a facial expression similar to those in photos they take of you dropping down on the giant roller coaster at Six Flags.

His tail was tucked between his back legs like a dog scared to death. His nostrils flared as they slowed; I assumed this was probably the first breath he had taken since Boog broke sixty-five miles per hour. His mane was standing straight up, filled with static electricity.

The horse never moved as the pickup came to a stop. It was as if he was frozen solid. I examined the lacerations and decided to suture the horse on the trailer. I never sedated him; I just put a local block on the skin to keep it from hurting and went to work. He never moved. Occasionally that horse would look down at me as if to say, "Would you please buy me from this man so I won't have to ride this thing back home?"

But ride home, he did. They pulled out of the parking lot at 5:30 p.m., heading straight back to Memphis. By the time I had finished, there must have been twenty-five people standing around watching. It doesn't take long for news like that to spread in small towns. Everyone wanted to get there in time to see Boog and his rented U-Haul head home. I just have to wonder what the drivers who passed him on the highway must have thought.

# Moment 7

*Pappy Can Run*

I stood looking at him over the back of that studhorse, wondering if he was kidding or if he really thought it could happen.

Not everyone sees the world the same way, and some people have misconceptions of what might happen in certain situations. But this question moved to the front of the list: do people really think that way?

The question surfaced at the end of a detailed story about his studhorse, Pappy Can Run. With a name like that, you would think that everyone would want to breed his or her mare to him, but it just wasn't happening. Last year, he could get only eight mares booked to breed to ol' Pappy, and after long hours of consideration, he had decided why.

Seems that the year before last, Pappy bred twelve mares, and four of them wound up aborting twins. As fate would have it, three of the eight bred last year aborted twins, too. I have to admit that the odds of that happening are astronomical, but still, it was just bad luck.

There was no convincing Pappy's owner of that, though. He had spent eight months contemplating the situation and had come up with a solution.

How many ideas must have gone through that fellow's head before he came up with this one? He must have spent countless hours wondering why no one wanted to breed to Pappy, and then once he decided on the reason, he must have spent days and days coming up with a solution.

The real reason was, well...Pappy just wasn't very good. He was a bit swaybacked, kind of short in the pastern, and a bit jug-headed. He had a bad slope in the shoulder and a left front leg that was a mite crooked, but most of all, he was slower than molasses. I guess that fellow just loved Pappy so much that he couldn't see those shortcomings, so it had to be something else.

And that "something else" was the twinning problem. Yep, that had to be it. Because in this fellow's eyes, Pappy was the perfect specimen. It had to be that the owners of all the really fast mares were afraid that Pappy was throwing too many twins.

He had arrived at a solution. Yes, he had deliberated endlessly on how to solve the twinning problem. What he came up with never would have crossed my mind, but it was first on his list of things that would fix the twinning dilemma and get Pappy more mares to breed than he could handle.

The solution was found in the question. That's right; the question held the answer that would make all future breedings of Pappy a guaranteed single live foal. So what did he ask me after all that big, long history on why no one wanted to breed to the famous studhorse, Pappy Can Run?

"So, Doc, don't you think it would fix everything if we removed just one of his testicles?"

# Moment 8

*Jimmy Stewart*

I guess one of my favorite things about being a veterinarian is helping in the process of bringing a new critter into the world.

After more than ten years and thousands of deliveries, it still stirs a special sentiment within me.

It must be a strange thought in a little calf's mind to look up and see a big nose, moustache, and glasses as the opening act in the play of life. But, as with most things, I don't get to see them unless there's a problem.

It was an average afternoon when the phone rang. A local rancher's heifer was having trouble calving.

This guy reminded me of Jimmy Stewart. He had the same sound to his voice and moved his head and neck like Mr. Stewart did. It made it a lot of fun to be around him. I've been here long enough to know most of the people around who have livestock, and I know how they like to do things. When this fellow couldn't get the calf out himself, I knew it was going to be a doozy. And sure enough, it was.

The calf was twisted and presenting upside down. For those of you who have not had the privilege of trying to pull a seventy-five-pound baby out of a small-hipped heifer, I will give you a couple of analogies: it is sorta like doing a carburetor job through the tailpipe or pulling a marshmallow out of a piggy bank.

We got this heifer into the chute and started the tedious process of straightening out the calf. I worked on it for about half an hour and then got a total body cramp and had to take a breather.

Upon seeing this, Jimmy just hopped in and spelled me. He pulled and twisted, moaned and sputtered, and finally tagged off to me again. By now, the heifer had lain down and was not even attempting to help by pushing. We were both covered with that sticky cow juice that comes with birth. It is God's WD-40, and boy, is it slick! In fact, if you step in cow juice in an unfocused moment, you will slide as if you are on ice, flinging your arms to maintain balance and looking as old as you are getting.

After you have done this for a while, your temper is on a hair trigger.

Over the years, I have developed the ability to do this while talking on the phone, answering questions from other clients, and lining up appointments for tomorrow. Mr. Stewart, on the other hand, was used to doing this without spectators. Most of the time at the vet clinic, someone will be standing around with the "Cliff Clavin" mentality. This, of course, means they have seen it all and done it all.

This day was no exception. Some fellow I had not seen before and haven't seen since showed up and started watching.

It was Jimmy's turn again when this guy walked up. Mr. Stewart was engulfed in one of those heavy straining moments when this spectator suddenly says, "I had an aunt who could just walk out into the field and pull one of those things out."

Now, I have heard those things ever since I started being a vet. It bounced right off me. I just figured this spectator had no idea what he was talking about, and he was giving us a demonstration of his ignorance. I had no idea that Jimmy was paying any attention at all. Just about the time that Mr. Stewart got the calf untwisted, he lost his grip, and the calf recoiled to the very position it was in when we started about an hour earlier. Frustration was at an all-time high. I told him to take a break and let me have another shot at it.

Once again, the spectator started. This time he said, "She could have really done good if she would have had one of these fancy things to catch the cow in."

Once again, the comment just bounced off me. But much to my surprise, when I looked up at the normally mild-mannered Jimmy, his face was beet red, and a puff of smoke was coming out of each ear.

"It's not that easy, you see," Jimmy said with a vintage Stewart accent. "This calf is all twisted up, you see."

If you will picture Jimmy Stewart in *It's a Wonderful Life*, you will see in your mind just exactly what this guy looked like.

"If she is so good at this, why don't you just go and get her?" he finally said.

Upon hearing this, the spectator turned and left. I have no idea who he was. I don't know if I was just simpled out or if it was really that funny, but I got to laughing so hard that I had to quit pulling and just lie there in the cow juice, producing that laugh that doesn't even make any noise.

Jimmy apologized, saying, "I hope I didn't run off any of your clients."

I told him not to worry.

We finally got the calf out and went on with life. I often think about that moment, about Jimmy standing there, covered with the slickest substance in the world—it was even in his hair, making it stick straight up—red-faced, sleeves rolled up, frustrated beyond words, telling the spectator to just go and get that aunt.

Oh, by the way, she never showed up.

# *fourteen*

## Old Women

# Moment 1

### Thermometer

"Pampered" was a patient early in my practice career. I've never felt so sorry for an animal in all my life. Who names a dog Pampered? I'll tell you who—people who are planning on doing just that. This critter spent its entire life being doted on and fussed over to the point that I think it had brain damage.

Pampered belonged to a sixty-year-old couple, Freeda and Dick. You know these people. Their precious dog required every ounce of obsessive behavior they could muster. Anal-retentive small-dog owners drive me crazy!

It was a Sunday morning, about 5:00 a.m., when the phone rang and the unbelievable string of questions came up that would characterize my relationship with these people for twelve more years.

"Dr. Brock, this is Freeda. Pam-Pam is sick. She has been up all night pacing and is distressed. I really need to take her temperature, and I have four lubricants I can use on the thermometer: K-Y Jelly, Vaseline, Panolog, or honey. Which one would you recommend?"

I was sound asleep. Do you know how hard it is to go from being sound asleep to answering a question like that? In fact, I couldn't come up with an answer. I wasn't even sure if I was awake or dreaming. But Freeda cleared her throat a few times during the extended pause, which convinced me that silence wasn't going to make the situation go away, so I started speaking.

Now, I was speaking before I was really awake, and some of the things I said were just as much a surprise to me as they must have been to her. It was as if my brain had taken over in a weird, parasympathetic way and was having its own conversation with this woman while I just listened.

"You were actually considering using honey on something you are going to stick up a rectum?" My voice had an overtone of disgust that was unintended. I'm not sure why my brain did it, but it didn't stop there.

"Do you stick the thermometer in the honey jar or pour the honey on it?" I asked. "Isn't that a little too sticky a substance to be considered a lubricant? Have you used honey in a fanny before? Where did you even get the idea to use honey? Did your mother do that to you?" It was almost as if I couldn't stop asking her questions. Yet, she never answered any of them.

I was beginning to wake up, and the more awake I became, the more I remembered whom I was talking to. If Freeda even sort of perceived that she had done something to endanger Pam-Pam, she was going to come apart.

"Oh my God, I am so glad I called you," Freeda declared. "Dick suggested the honey, and I personally thought it was a bad idea. He did say his mother used honey on the thermometer, but it was an oral thermometer. Would it have killed Pam-Pam if we'd used it? I am just so glad we called." She hung up without even saying good-bye.

I, too, hung up the phone and rolled over to go back to sleep. My wife wasn't going to let that happen, though.

"Who were you just talking to?" she asked. "Did you just ask them about sticking something in a rectum? I thought I heard you ask them about using honey as a lubricant for sticking something in a rectum. Is that what I heard you say? Wake up."

Ten minutes later, after explaining all about Freeda and Dick, I couldn't go back to sleep. I'm still not completely sure which lubricant they used, but I'm sure it wasn't honey.

# Moment 2

*Fat Dog*

It seems like we humans just can't help it; we have a need to care for things. It is this deep-seated need that makes dogs fat. I'll bet three out of five little dogs that come into the clinic are overweight. It is an honest mistake. The owners are just trying to satisfy their pets.

Have you ever just stopped for a second in the dog food aisle and read the packaging descriptions?

Succulent beef and chicken

No by-products

Tender morsels of bacon and cheese

Beef stew

Tasty pieces of real pork

Lamb and rice in hearty gravy

Hamburger patties

No wonder we have so many fat dogs; they eat better than we do. But the fact is, it is not the dog food that makes 'em fat; it is the table food. Those tidbits and morsels that we just can't help picking from the dinner table add up to major calories for our friends.

I am standing at the exam table, looking at a fifteen-pound Chihuahua (which should weigh six pounds), and discussing the health risks of having a fat dog.

This dog looks like a walking coffee table. The owner says the usual: "She doesn't eat much at all." I'm thinking that this would be the equivalent of me weighing about four hundred pounds. You can't tell me that I'm getting up to four hundred pounds without eating too much.

It takes some skilled questioning to get the truth, and it's a challenge—almost like being a detective. As the conversation proceeds, I find that the dog eats only a few morsels of dog food a day.

When asked about table food, the reply is: "We don't give them anything from the table while we are eating."

All right, does this dog get any other food besides the few morsels of dog food a day?

"Well, I fix it two strips of bacon and an egg every morning," is the low-volume reply that fills the air.

Think about that. When you compare consumption by weight, this would be like me eating forty strips of bacon and twenty eggs for breakfast every morning. What do you think? Would this add a little more depth to my belly button?

Other people have strange conceptions of what food really is. I am standing at the table again looking at an obese poodle. I have asked questions from every angle that I can think of to determine what is causing this dog to be so fat. Even the trickiest questions find the owner still convinced that the dog has a problem with its hormones. She swears that the dog never eats scraps or human food of any type. I am just about convinced that there may be a problem other than table scraps; then, the dog starts retching. After a few heaves, a blob of substance flies out of its mouth and lands on the table. Further inspection reveals a few chocolate chips and some doughy material.

"I thought you said this rascal doesn't eat any human food," I said as I picked up the pile.

"That's cookie dough," she replied. "The dog just loves it. It's not food until you cook it; is it?"

What do you think? Is raw cookie-dough food? Would you ever think that anyone considered things that were not cooked to be something other than food?

Other things make it very difficult to discuss obesity. Tell me this, how do you tell a four hundred–pound owner that his or her dog is too fat? Now, that is a touchy subject. You certainly don't want to hurt his or her feelings, but dogs were not made to be fat. We humans can handle it much better than they can.

My favorite description of fat dogs is: "We are killing them with kindness." We don't mean to jeopardize their health; we just want them to be happy. So, the next time you learn that a client feeds his or her ten-pound dog a strip of bacon, remind him or her that it would be like eating fifteen or twenty strips.

# Moment 3

*Chew*

The human-animal bond is a strong one, and at times, I am amazed at what people will do for their animals.

I know people who will buy their pets an ice-cream cone before coming to see me. I've seen painted toenails, dogs with pierced ears, cats with a gold-capped tooth, dogs with rollers in their hair, many types of sweaters, a horse with a glass eye, bunk beds for cats, various types of tattoos on pets, an artificial testicle placed back in the scrotum to keep it from looking empty, tubal ligations and vasectomies so the animals can still have fun but not get pregnant, wheelchairs for paraplegic dachshunds, contact lenses for poor vision in old dogs, tennis shoes for hunting dogs, and on and on.

But I have never seen anything like what happened a few months back.

The presenting complaint was that this dog "just can't chew food." The dog was a burly bulldog that slobbered continuously. Just looking at the critter, you could not tell anything was wrong. The dog just stood there panting and slobbering all over everything in sight. The little lady who brought the creature in was obviously in love with this drooling rascal. The look in her eyes was nothing less than terror.

It seemed that ol' bulldog, Bule, had been unable to eat for a while. When I asked what the problem seemed to be, she just shook her head and said, "He hasn't been able to chew his food for about three weeks now."

179

This rascal was fat and sassy. He certainly did not look like he had gone without food for three weeks. Besides that, why did she wait so long to bring him in if things were so destitute?

"Something is terribly wrong with his chewing mechanism," was the statement she made over and over as I examined the jowls of this spit factory.

The more I looked, the more it became apparent the ol' Bule had a dislocated joint in his jaw. When his mouth closed, the teeth did not line up anymore.

I was amazed. How could this fat critter have made it so long without being able to chew? He could lick, though. Boy, he could lick. His tongue was about four inches wide and must have been ten inches long. He loved to use it. The entire time I was examining him, he was licking his nose and my face. No matter where I moved, he could stick that thing out and give my cheek a good licking. By the time I was through with the exam, I had Bule spit in my moustache, all over my glasses, in both nostrils, in my ear holes, and all over my hat.

"How have you kept this dog from drying up and blowing away?" I asked as I pondered the condition of the dog.

"Well, I kept thinking he would get better on his own. When it first happened, I thought it would get better, but it just hasn't. I just couldn't stand to see him take a bite of food and then watch it just fall back out of his mouth. So, I decided that I would just chew his food for him while whatever was wrong got better. I would just chew the food myself and then put it in his mouth. Some of it would fall back out, but most of it he was able to swallow."

I was mesmerized by the thought of this little woman chewing every bite of Bule's food for the last three weeks. She must have chewed it for a while and then spit it back into her hand before she poked it down his throat. I was trying to picture it all in my mind as she went on with the story.

"It didn't seem to bother him a bit for me to chew the food first. But don't you worry, Dr. Brock. I know better than to feed him human food. You told me a long time ago to never feed Bule human food, so I chewed his dog food, hoping that it would have everything in it he needed to get well."

Well now, what would you have done at this point?

I was just amazed. Do you realize how much dog food you would have to chew a day to keep a fifty-pound bulldog in good shape? Can you imagine doing that for three weeks? What must her breath have smelled like? Why didn't she just get canned food? I started to go get a bowl of dog food for her to show me the entire procedure, but I decided that everyone might just get sick watching.

We fixed ol' Bule, and he went on to do just fine. I decided that this was the greatest act of owner loyalty that I had ever witnessed. Man, what a job.

*fifteen*

## Cowgirls

# Cowgirls

Like many things, the definition of cowgirls has changed over time. I remember my great-grandparents well and spent a lot of time with them. I cannot speak for the rest of America, but where I grew up, the women did not do much on horseback. They were most often cooking and cleaning and keeping the home going.

This changed as each generation passed. I never saw my grandfather's sisters ride a horse. I never saw my mother ride a horse. But the days of women staying home and not working on the ranch have gone. Women now are right in the middle of calf workings and horsemanship.

This generation of cowgirls is tough and ready. They know horses as well or better than a lot of men and are woven into the fabric of what the modern-day ranch is all about. They have a perspective. It is one that has come with the liberation of the modern world, determination, hard work, and trials. Some of my favorite clients are cowgirls. They are wonderful.

# Moment 1

## Stage Chicken

Some things in this life just aggravate, occurring with no rhyme or reason, like a bad dream or a pimple. Rude name-calling is one of them, regardless of what they say about sticks and stones.

Mrs. Peterson and I were in the clinic's equine center, ultrasounding a tendon on her studhorse. He was lame, and we were intently looking at the flexor tendon, trying to determine how bad the lesion was and what we should do to make him better.

It was one of those rare occasions when it was just two of us and the patient inside the barn.

About ten minutes into the exam, a loud, rather repulsive voice bellowed out from some distance away, echoing off everything.

I was under this twelve-hundred–pound animal and could feel its muscles tighten as the scary voice struck its ears. The bent-over position I was in left little option for a quick exit. If this horse lunged, it was going to step on some part of me that certainly can't stand twelve hundred pounds of pressure. But, just before it came to full attention, I was up and happy that my leg was still attached to my body.

"Hello in there. How is everybody doooooooing today? It's great to see you," this fellow screamed, like a high-pressure salesman in a late-night infomercial. His words bounced off the rafters.

I looked across the room to see a man who looked like he'd spent ten years working at a carnival. His matted hair hung to his shoulders, his face was covered with long, thin hair that collectively gave him the appearance of a mange-laden collie, and his clothes were covered with stains.

My heart was still pounding, and I was feeling a touch of anger as I stammered for something to say that would reflect my anger without being too rude.

Before I could speak, he droned, "I represent the [XYZ] Beef Co—"

I interrupted him right there, before his screaming put the stud-horse into fight-or-flight mode.

"We are working on horses in here, and they get frightened by loud voices."

My interruption didn't faze him. Instead, he interrupted me again in the same obnoxious way.

"And I was just wondering if you might be needing anything today?"

"Sir, what we need is for you to be quiet and just go away," I replied, just as the horse began to dance around with flared nostrils and big eyes. I had passed the point of being nice, adding a tone of authority to my voice.

He just continued in the same loud manner, but his next words left Mrs. Peterson and me with dropped jaws.

Looking back, it must have taken this fellow a moment to absorb the fact that I was trying to get him to leave as he continued with his thought process.

But finally he blurted out, "We have steak and chicken, and f--- you!" The words rolled out of his carnie mouth as he turned and got back into his little white pickup with a freezer in the bed.

I caught the two-word obscenity, but somehow, my ears did not hear "steak and chicken."

I thought the man had just called me a stage chicken. I had never heard that term before.

Judging by the two words that followed, I guessed that stage chicken must be a terrible thing to call someone. I was furious that he'd called me a stage chicken in front of a lady. I had no idea what it meant but could feel my ears turning red with anger.

"That was so terrible. I'm sorry you had to hear that. I've never been called that before, don't really even know what it means," I said to Mrs. Peterson in my most heartfelt, apologetic tone.

But Mrs. Peterson had heard it correctly. She knew the man had said "steak and chicken," so she assumed I was talking about the last two words he uttered—the expletive.

Her face had a strange, almost twisted look.

"You have never heard that before?" she asked. "I thought everyone in the world had heard that by the time they were your age. I don't use that kind of language, but I have certainly heard those two words."

My mind went into overdrive. This woman had heard "stage chicken" and seemed to know it was a derogatory term. How could I be forty-five years old without ever hearing anyone called a stage chicken? Yet this nice woman assumed that everyone knew what a stage chicken was. I didn't want to compound my ignorance, so I just went back to work on the horse.

Shortly after, Dr. Michelle came into the room and started helping with the exam. She noticed my ears and face were red and must have sensed my anger. In a compassionate voice, she asked if I felt OK.

"Did you just see that carnie-looking dude who was standing at the door, screaming at us to buy his products?" I asked.

"No. What are you talking about?"

"There was a man here trying to sell something out of the back of his truck, screaming from that door over there. He spooked this horse and called me a stage chicken."

"A what?"

"A stage chicken. He called me a stage chicken. Mrs. Peterson said she has heard of it, and that everyone else in the world has, too. I guess I've been living in a vacuum all these years, because I don't know what it means, but it really ticked me off. This guy looked like he hadn't bathed in ten years. I'm not sure I like being called a stage chicken by someone like him."

Mrs. Peterson started to laugh.

She explained that he had said "steak and chicken" and that she thought I was talking about the second two words.

We all laughed about it for the rest of the day. In fact, we still laugh and call each other stage chicken every now and then.

# Moment 2

### *Tammy*

S ometimes you just need to stop and think. You know what I am talk-ing about; some moments in the practice of veterinary medicine require a tremendous amount of contemplation. It is during these mo-ments that a little peace and quiet would be nice.

Lameness exams often evoke this contemplation requirement for me. Unlocking the mystery of an upper-hind-end lameness in a horse requires some thought. I enjoy doing these exams, but I have been known to sneak off to my office for a few minutes to assimilate the clues that I've accumulated in order to make a logical decision on what the problem is or what should be done. The harder the lameness, the more quiet I require.

Tammy is a five-foot-tall, ball-of-fire barrel-racer. She has some world-class horses and is a blast to be around. When she shows up with a lameness, it is usually a subtle one that requires my full concentration. The problem with that is that Tammy is a talker.

When I say she is a talker, I mean this little gal can't stand a moment of silence. It is almost as if she has a pathological aversion to being in the presence of others when no conversation is occurring. She will see to it that something is being said all the time, and most of the time, she does it with questions. This means that you have to be involved in the process of stamping out quiet with her.

This particular day found me working up a very difficult lameness for her. I was digging deep into my gray matter, trying to piece together the clues of why her seven-year-old gelding was three-tenths of a sec-ond off. It just wasn't flowing. Every time I would begin to ponder the results of the last portion of the exam, she would sense that things were too quiet and hammer me with a volley of questions. Eeeesh!

The last thing I wanted to do was hurt her feelings by asking her to be quiet, so I began looking around for something that would occupy her for a little while as I thought about the problem at hand. She was rambling on about some horse she had ridden ten years ago that acted a little like this one when it occurred to me that her constantly moving hands were a vital part of her talking arsenal. I began to wonder what would happen if I could somehow still those hands. Would it stop the talking?

As she entered the fifth or sixth paragraph about the horse from ten years ago, I simply handed her an empty syringe case. She never stopped talking or moving her hands; she simply accepted it and continued on with the story without so much as a comma. Next, I handed her an empty bottle of Carbocaine, which she gladly accepted with her other hand and just rolled right on with the story.

This was actually getting kinda fun. I was beginning to wonder how many things she would hold before she actually looked down to see what they were. So I handed her a pair of hoof testers. This stopped the chatter momentarily. The hoof testers were heavier, and there was no readily empty hand to hold them. So she took them, placed them under her left arm, and continued with the story.

I maintained eye contact with her and inserted occasional head movements to make her feel as if I was listening intently to her story, but just kept handing her things. Next, it was an earpiece from an otoscope that was setting next to me on the counter. After that, an extension set, still in the package. Next was a digital thermometer and the case it came in. She was still going with the story, but her tempo had slowed down just a bit. It was now becoming almost impossible to move her hands, which obviously was causing the conversation cortex in her brain to sputter a bit.

I stopped handing her stuff for a second to see if she would ever pause and notice all meaningless things she was holding for me.

Nope.

Time to hand some more. There was little room left to accept things. She had arranged them in various places to make holding them easier but still had no idea what she was holding. Next, it was a package of 2-0 Vicryl, still in the plastic. Then a pair of rubber gloves that I had just taken off. Not enough? How about a three-inch-tall stack of four-by-four gauze?

This finally stopped all ability to move the hands. She now had enough stuff that she had to hold some of it mashed between her arms and tummy. When this happened, all talking came to a standstill. But she still had never even looked to see what all I had given her.

A few moments passed with no noise coming from either of us. I just stood there looking at her and finally couldn't maintain a straight face. She asked why I was giggling.

"Thanks for holding all that for me," kinda trickled out the corner of my now-laughing mouth.

She looked down and assessed what all she had taken from me. She started laughing, too. And pretty soon, we were both laughing so hard that others in the clinic came over to find out what had happened.

"I guess you figured out that I can't talk if I don't move my hands. Well, I was just getting to the good part of that story when you handed me all this stuff," she said as she started to set it all down on the counter.

"Oh, no!" I bellered out before she could get her hands empty. "You have to hold all that until I have had enough quiet time to figure out what is wrong with your horse. Then you can set it all down and start telling me the story again!"

Every time she comes to the clinic now, I greet her with an armful of meaningless stuff and tell her if she can't be quiet, she is gonna have to hold it all until I am done.

# Moment 3

*Etti*

I had heard about these people ever since I arrived in Lamesa. They lived in New Mexico and had a huge number of horses. The husband was the rodeo coach at the university and knew as much about horses as anyone I had ever met. I believe the hardest thing one can do as a veterinarian is break into the horse world. And I wanted to be a horse doctor.

My first year in Lamesa after buying the practice, I saw ninety-six horses. That is ninety-six the entire year. Last year, we saw eight thousand. But I had no idea it would ever lead to this. I really wanted to impress the rodeo coach from Hobbs, New Mexico, because I figured he would send me a lot of good horses.

He called me on a Tuesday and said he had seven horses that needed a good vet. I was so excited. I told him to come on over, and we would do whatever we could to make those horses happy. He replied that he would be busy, but he would load them and send his wife over. He said she would be there about one o'clock Texas time, and he would appreciate a call when I figured each one of them out.

I was so excited I nearly peed my pants. This was the break I had been looking for, and I did not want to mess it up. I spent all of Monday readying the clinic for a newfound client. My second year of having the practice in Lamesa was going better than the first, but it was still miles from what I was hoping for.

One o'clock Tuesday arrived, but there was no sign of Etti Bess (his wife). I was going over in my mind the conversation he and I'd had a few days earlier and wondering if I had said something to make him

195

mad. Two o'clock arrived, and still no Etti Bess. I was beginning to think that I had truly irked him. You have to remember, this is occurring at a time when almost no one had a cell phone yet, and I really had no way to talk to him or her.

Three o'clock arrived, and still no horses. I was devastated. I went over our conversation a thousand times in my head and just couldn't find anything about it that was negative. Two hours late usually means not coming at all, so I gave up and pouted for a while.

About three thirty, a truck with a long trailer slowly pulled into the parking lot at Brock Vet Clinic. A pretty woman, about thirty-five years old, got out and came strolling toward me. She looked upset and dismayed.

"You will never believe how terrible my trip over here was!" she said with absolute conviction in her voice.

"I stopped at the convenience store on the west side of Lamesa when I got into town to get a Coke. I parked on the south side of the store and went in to go to the bathroom and get a drink. Well, it seems I forgot to put on the emergency brake when I got out. Do you know how heavy a Ford dually and seven horses are? I mean, I never thought to put on the emergency brake. I guess after I got out, the pickup started rolling. Well, I know it did. And it rolled across the street. And then up into a yard. And then through the front wall of this man's house. And then into his living room. And through the living room and into the kitchen. And then through the kitchen and into the bedroom. But at least it stopped there. He was asleep on the couch in the living room—you know, he works nights. But anyway, it didn't hit him at all. But when he woke up, the trailer with all the horses was in his living room. He said that was quite startling. I can see why. I never thought you could back a pickup with a trailer out of a house, but you can. Anyway, I am late because all that happened. But I think everything is OK now. He was in his underwear. When I came out of the store, I thought someone had stolen my truck. I was about to call the police when I saw my trailer sticking out from the front of that house. So anyway, here is a list of what is wrong with the horses. Sorry again that I am late."

I can remember thinking how calm this woman was for just running through a house. I went over to the pickup and found stucco from the house's exterior stuck in the grill and windshield wipers. I couldn't imagine being so calm after such an experience, but this woman was ice.

We went on to become good friends. I have worked on their horses for twenty years, and every time Etti Bess comes over, I have to ask if she drove through a house to get here.

# Moment 4

*Toot*

I had been working on her horse for several hours, trying to figure out why it was limping. It was one of those really tough lamenesses that requires all of the patience one can muster up and then some. Thank goodness she was a fun-loving, happy person who was interesting to visit with and anxious to help.

It was during one of those ten-minute waiting periods between diagnostic nerve blocks that she decided to tell me a joke. We are about the same age, and it was some joke about kids and getting older, but I really don't remember the joke at all. In fact, I didn't think the joke was one bit funny.

But she did. She told the joke and began laughing and laughing. I normally like it when people laugh at their own jokes, but she laughed way too hard. In fact, she laughed so hard that she tooted. Yep, she tooted. It was just me and her standing there, and she had just tooted in C-sharp. What is a person to do?

Here is a brief recap of what went through my mind: That lady just tooted. I am now horribly uncomfortable and have no idea what to do. Just calm down a second, and don't change expressions. Let her make the first move. Maybe she thinks I didn't hear it? No, that was way too loud; all the horses looked over to see who did it. Resist the urge to step away from her, and don't breathe in for a minute or so.

Should I just say something now and get it over with? I could make a joke out of it, and she would probably just laugh along with me. Let me check out the expression on her face. Yeah, that will tell me if she is embarrassed or ready to joke about it...Nope, she is not looking too joke-worthy right this second. In fact, I think she is turning red.

Oh my, I need to do something to make her feel comfortable. Maybe I should laugh at the stupid joke now. Maybe I should toot, too, and then she would feel better about her toot.

No, we need something else to take our attention...something that will just move us on to the next subject, and we can act as if nothing ever happened. Come on, Bo. Come on. Think of something to talk about. Any other time you could think of a topic to talk about in a millisecond. Why do you have to freeze up under pressure?

Suddenly, I am feeling the urge to laugh. Don't do it. But that was an amazingly high-pitched toot that must have lasted a full second. You could have tuned a guitar off the purity of that note. Bahahahahahahaha. No, no, no, just think about something that is not funny at all...baseball, cryptorchid pigs, fishing shows on TV, having to set through *The Nutcracker* last Christmas. Yeah, yeah, that's working. I am losing the laugh urge...

As luck would have it, one of the other doctors came around the corner and asked me a question. Oh my, I have never latched on to a question so quick as that one. In fact, I instantly answered and even said we needed to go to the other barn and check it out.

I came back in about fifteen minutes, and everything was OK. She looked composed again, and we went right back to working up the lameness in her horse. Wow, what a moment.

# Moment 5

*Ass Spavin*

There are just some things that you cannot learn in school. Some situations cry out for more than learning and science. This was one of them. All I knew about the woman was that she was from San Angelo, and she had a barrel-racing horse that was lame. I had no idea that the episode that was about to occur was going to require every ounce of tact I could muster up and actually leave me at a loss for words. Unbelievable.

Six people crawled out of the bowels of the giant dually pickup that pulled the brand-new three-horse slant. I was guessing that the entire rig had cost about $70,000. Wow. Here they were, the woman who was the barrel-racer, her husband, her sister, her sister's husband, and both of her parents. As I watched the unloading process from the back door of the clinic, it became painfully obvious that this woman was bossy. She had brought all of these people and had a job for each of them. It was like a military drill as she assigned each one a task and saw to it that those tasks were done to the very last detail.

As I entered the scene with a handshake and introduction, she gave me a slight smile and then went directly into a detailed description of what was "ailing" the horse. It seemed that the only complaint was that the horse was not running as fast as it had last year. In other words, it was about a half of a second slower this year than it was at the same races last year. Her "crew" had saddled the horse, and she was promptly on board, still talking as she trotted off.

No one else in the entire group had uttered a word up to this point. They gathered around and looked closely at me while I looked at the horse. It was as if they were watching my face for any change in emotion or expression. It was making me a little nervous. They were so focused on me that I was startin' to wonder if I had a booger or something stuck to a tooth.

"How long has this critter been lame?" I asked as I wiped my arm across my nose and sniffed.

The spokesman of the group seemed to be the brother-in-law.

He replied, "Ha, that's what we wonder." I had no idea what that meant.

The pressure of the situation was rising as I discovered that I couldn't see anything wrong with the horse. I had watched the woman trot around the parking lot for what seemed like ten minutes, and that horse had not taken a lame step. The pressure went up even more when the brother-in-law informed me that I was the fourth vet she had brought the horse to.

I was hoping they would give me some kind of hint as to what the other vets had said was wrong with the horse, but they just stood there and stared at me as I watched the horse. Not wanting to disappoint them, I finally stated, "Well, he sure might have a little bone spavin." I figured this was a safe guess; nearly every barrel horse in the world has some degree of it. It is an arthritis that develops in the hock.

As these words left my lips, I began returning their stares to see if my statement stirred any emotions. To my surprise, it seemed to rustle up a disgusted look on each of their faces.

The spokesman brother-in-law said, "That horse ain't got no bone spavin. If he has any kind of spavin, it's ass spavin."

Once again, I had no idea what that was. Nine years of being a veterinarian and I had never heard of that one or read about it in any of the literature. Not wanting to look stupid, I continued to watch the horse trot endlessly around the parking lot. I began thinking perhaps it was something the horse had caught from a donkey. After all, ass spavin sounded a little mulish or even a touch anal. I was wondering if I had missed that lecture in vet school. The brother-in-law had said it so confidently that it must have been a term that the family had heard somewhere.

I was digging for some way to ask questions and gather clues without appearing uninformed. Finally, I asked, "Which leg is it in?"

To this, the brother-in-law stated, "It ain't in no leg. Tell him what the deal is, Robby."

Everyone gathered in even closer as Robby, the husband, began to explain the situation. "You see, Dr. Brock, my wife has gained about twenty pounds in the last year or so. We know that there is nothing wrong with that horse; it just can't carry the extra weight as fast. We heard that you were good at explaining things and hoped that you could tell her; none of us has the guts to."

All I could do now was look at her pronounced muffin top as she trotted the horse in circles. What page of my notes from vet school should I turn to for the answer to this dilemma? My mind became numb as my face became red. Two hours these people drove just to put me in this situation. They were all afraid of her, and I was finding myself scared to death of her also. What in the world was this bossy momma going to do when I told her the horse was fine; she was just too thick? *"That's right, bigun, you lose some tons, and this critter will be at least a half a second faster."*

Two hours these people drove, and now there I stood, sweating. What would you have done?

# Moment 6

*Thong?*

When I was a kid, flip-flops were called thongs. But these days, the latter term refers almost exclusively to a certain type of undergarment. It took several years and a collection of raised eyebrows and awkward stares to retool my vocabulary, but I eventually made the transition.

And although images of almost any beach suggest the two go together like peas and carrots, sometimes they just don't mix.

She was about nineteen years old. I had never met her before, and after the embarrassment that was about to unfold, I wouldn't expect to see her again.

She came up to the back of the clinic, leading a horse while detailing a problem it had with a tooth. She stopped walking at the back door but proceeded to dictate a long history about the horse's speed, and she said that she surmised its decline in speed was due to its toothache.

She was a barrel-racer, and like the rest of them, she was greatly concerned with speed. But she was a bit different from the run-of-the-mill barrel-racers I had met.

It started with her wardrobe. It wasn't the cowgirl outfit that most donned. She was wearing a denim skirt, a lacy, green, baby-doll T-shirt, a pair of flip-flops, and an undergarment that left very little to the imagination. Curious about how I know that? Keep reading.

She continued to tell me about this supposed tooth problem as I motioned toward the stocks so she could secure the horse, and I could start my exam. She continued to talk as she walked in front of the horse to change its direction, but her mouth was moving faster than her feet.

I looked down at the exact moment that the horse's right front foot landed on the back of her left flip-flop. This set off a remarkable chain of events, beginning with me lunging forward to catch her.

Denim miniskirts do not stretch; they just move in the direction of least resistance. When a horse is standing on your left foot while the right foot is already overstretched forward, that direction is up. The farther apart her legs split, the faster the skirt rose toward her waist.

I didn't have time to calculate the physics of it as I reached to break her fall, but the flailing arms and separating feet left little to take hold of.

The horse politely stopped when it saw its handler was in trouble, but it didn't move off her sandal. Her hanging on to the lead kept her from going down completely, but it might have been better if she did.

Here is the scene: There is a nineteen-year-old girl wearing a miniskirt around her midchest as she props herself on one knee and two forearms while keeping her left foot squarely on the ground, thanks to a thousand-pound horse. It looks like an impromptu game of Twister, minus the colored dots and happy faces.

I bailed out on trying to catch her for fear of taking embarrassment to a whole, new level. We both froze for a second in that position as we tried to figure a way to untangle this mess. Finally, the horse took a step back, and she sprang onto her back and then onto her feet, tugging down on the hem of her skirt that was gathered around her chest.

What do you say to a perfect stranger who just rolled into a ball of near nakedness in front of you? Nothing. We just continued as if nothing had happened.

We did the work-up on the horse, and I treated it as best I could. She paid the bill, jumped in her truck, and I have never seen her since.

That might be the day that thongs and flip-flops took on two completely different meanings for me. And I realized there would be times when the two just don't mix.

*sixteen*

## Cowboys

# Cowboys

These are the people I watched as I grew up. I will never say that I, myself, am a cowboy, but I idolized these men during my youth. These particular humans are amazing to me. They possess the perspective that I find to be the most interesting.

Perhaps I define a cowboy a little different than a purist would. These are men who work outside raising crops and livestock. They are the most creative and intelligent group I know. Just consider what they have accomplished over the last hundred or so years. Things such as tractors that can pull giant plows and produce abundant crops and cattle that can survive and thrive to make the beef we eat. If you have ever been around cowboys, you will understand that they have a way of doing things that is unlike any other.

Most of them can repair or produce just about anything that is needed to keep a ranch running. They can weld and build with wood. They can string fence for miles. They can deliver calves and keep horses sound. They can stand the hottest and coldest conditions Mother Nature has to offer. They seldom complain and hold a perspective of nature that often goes untold.

I have had the good fortune of knowing these people. I have spent countless hours in their company learning the mind-set of living off the land and respecting nature, with all of its beauty and wrath.

# Moment 1

*First C-section*

I was watching our oldest daughter, Emili, handle the wheel when she steered the car for the first time. At ten, she's been with us half the time she's going to be and is starting to grow up. We've always made driving look so easy, she probably assumed it was a snap. I had to move the wheel several times to keep us from hitting mailboxes and swerving into a ditch. After a few practice runs and some nervous moments, I'm sure she'll be fine. In a few more years, she'll be driving while talking on the phone, drinking a soda, and changing the radio station, all at the same time.

Her evolution of confidence reminded me of my first C-section on a cow.

I was in the thriving metropolis of Clarendon, Texas, surrounded by cowboys who had seen many more C-sections than I had. In fact, at three weeks postgraduation, I had never seen even one. This meant that the first one I was going to see was about to be done by me. Think about that, and then get nervous with me.

These weren't just any cowboys. They were from a ranch that had a reputation for being the best around. I was irked at my veterinary school for never in four years affording me the opportunity to see or do this procedure, although I did see it once on film.

The cowboys were sizing up the young Dr. Brock. They watched my every move, peering right through my artificial confidence. I was already half exhausted from trying to deliver the calf. I had pulled, poked, strained, twisted, lubricated, sweated, and groaned for about two hours. All the other veterinarians were gone, and there was no one to turn to except these fifteen guys, all of whom looked like the Marlboro Man. And, to make matters worse, they all thought I knew what I was doing.

The vet-school film showed the calf being delivered from the underside, with the cow on her back. I gathered from the cowboys that Dr. Deyhle performed C-sections through the left flank, with the cow standing.

What was I going to do? I'd never even seen a cow cut open in the flank, much less delivered a calf through that area. On the other hand, if they'd never seen one taken through the belly, they wouldn't know if I was messing up. Using that logic, I told them recent research had shown that the calf and cow did much better if the baby was taken through the belly, and, with no visible scar, cows usually sold better. This produced some low murmuring as they pondered the new idea. If there's one thing I've learned about people who live fifty miles from the nearest town, it is that anything new must be studied awhile before it is accepted.

After some high-level discussion among the oldest cowboys, it was decided the belly approach would be OK. We all knew that the calf was already dead. Apparently, they decided there wasn't much to lose.

They let the cow out of the chute, jumped on her, and in no time had her tied up and lying on her back. The stage was all mine. With trembling hands, I went to work. We put a local block in her belly, and I went to cutting. As sheer dumb luck would have it, the surgery went perfectly. I was in and out of that cow in about twenty minutes. She got up and went into the trailer as if nothing had ever happened.

The guys thought they'd just witnessed the newest thing in C-sections. As they drove off, I could hear them talking about the benefits of the "belly approach," and how great it was that there was no scar that would keep her from selling.

As for me, I was never so glad to be finished with anything in my life. I could feel the stomach juices churning away at the ulcer I was sure was forming. How many more of these "first-time-see-and-do" procedures would I have to endure?

I grew up a little that day. I never did another C-section through the belly of a cow for anyone but those ranchers and, if I can help it, I never will.

However, the veterinarian who does their work today tells me the cowboys insist that every C-section be done through the belly.

I finally got to see Dr. Deyhle do one with the cow standing. Boy, is it easier!

I guess we all have to nearly hit the mailbox and swerve a few times before we gain confidence.

I've done hundreds of C-sections over the years now. I can do them even while talking on the phone, drinking a soda, and changing the radio station.

# Moment 2

### Ricky and the Prolapse

It was a freezing cold day in February about thirty days after we first arrived in Lamesa. I still didn't really know anyone in town when Ricky pulled into the clinic with his father-in-law's prolapsed cow. She was in bad shape. Her uterus was hanging out and torn in several places. She was down in the trailer and could not get up.

Ricky came walking up with that smile that makes his eyes disappear and stated, "My name is Ricky, and I have a problem with this cow... Think you can fix her?"

Things didn't look too good, but I was young and eager to please. Since the cow couldn't get up, I went to work on her on the floor of the trailer. I was deep in thought, and deeper into the cow, when suddenly the trailer started moving. I looked up and could not see Ricky anywhere.

*What in the world is this guy doing?* raced through my mind as we started driving around the clinic. Was he driving off to run a few errands while I worked on his cow? His route took us around the clinic and back to the drive that leads to the garage door. The next thing I knew, we were backed into the clinic.

"I thought you looked a little cold and wet out there, so I pulled her in." This statement was followed by another eye-squinting grin and a jolly "yuk, yuk, yuk"-type laugh.

I was working like a sled dog—pushing, poking, tucking, and sliding. Nothing was working. The artery in the uterus had ruptured, and the uterus was filled with blood. This made it larger and more difficult to get back in. It also made the cow a bit "shocky."

About the time I was going to get up and tell Ricky that things were not looking too good, he said, "I think she quit breathing."

I bounded out of the trailer and got the epinephrine. After giving the shot, I jumped up and down on her chest for a while. I got the special mask and filled her lungs with oxygen. It was paying off. The cow began breathing again on her own.

When she looked stable, I began the arduous task of replacing the uterus again. By now, I was covered by blood, freezing to death, and running out of patience. Ricky just stood there and watched. I figured he was sizing up the new doctor, and as far as I could tell, I was not doing too well.

The more I pushed, the bigger that thing became. I would get one side in, and the other would pop out. I would push the middle in, and the sides would come back at me. It was the uterus that ate Manhattan, and, of course, it would have to happen the first time I met a new client.

Now my sweat was mixed with her blood. I lay back to take a breath, and Ricky whispered, "I think she is dead again."

Once again, I hopped up and sprinted into the clinic. I came out again with the same set of ER meds and went through the same dramatic actions. Once again, we were able to pull her from the clutches of death.

It was about an hour and a half into the ordeal when I lay back down and started trying to get the giant uterus back in its home. By now, the thing was nearly as big as the cow. It was not looking too good.

Ricky continued to watch with the eyes of a skeptic as I pushed and grunted. Once again, he whispered, "She's dead again."

I jumped up and headed for the medicine. This time, all the pumping and oxygen did no good. She was down for the count.

I was very disappointed and felt like a total failure. My face must have given away my feelings, because Ricky walked up and patted me on the back.

"Don't worry. If you don't have 'em, you can't lose 'em," were the words he chose to attempt to pick me up.

"Thanks. I guess you were sizing me up as I lay there and killed your cow. What did you come up with?" came rolling out of my mouth as we ambled into the clinic to warm up.

"Well, you are in some ways the same and in some ways different than the last vet that was here. You both kill every cow I bring ya. The difference is, it just takes you longer."

# Moment 3

*Vomit*

I'm forty now, and there just are not many things left to surprise me. I'm not saying I've seen it all, but most things fit into categories, and few things strike me as being unexpected. A few days ago, I did see something that was remarkable.

Working cattle is one of the last reminders of the Old West. In many ways, it has been done the same way for the last one hundred years. A few modern conveniences have entered the formula, like working alleys and squeeze chutes. A veterinarian's role in this well-orchestrated ritual is usually marked by palpating the cows for pregnancy. This entails wearing a plastic sleeve and running one's arm up the fanny to check for a calf in the womb.

This is a time when neighbors, day workers, and ranch hands get together to round up the cattle and run them through the chute to administer vaccinations and other annual necessities. The day worker is a crucial cog in the process. These people go from ranch to ranch and are paid on a per-day basis to assist in working cattle. These folks are quite a breed. They are about as rough and tough as they come, and they've seen it all.

We go to many of these workings each year, and every ranch has a little bit different way of getting the same jobs accomplished. It really doesn't matter to me how they do it, as long as they don't get me smushed or otherwise injured in the process. Most of the time, one of these day workers runs the squeeze chute. Typically, they draw a good amount of concern from my end. If they don't secure the cow well enough, she will back up and smash me against the gate. It has happened many times, and it often leads to a very hard time getting out of bed the next morning.

On this particular day, two day workers were running the chute. They were moving a bit slowly, perhaps from a bit of overindulgence the night before. They appeared to be a little green around the gills. I guess a few beers in the evening must soften some of the pain from a hard day in the saddle, but this pair likely had had more than a few.

The cowboys at the back of the line hollered, "Lumpy jaw!" as the old Hereford cow entered the chute. This is a condition that causes an accumulation of puss around the bottom-jaw area. It is pretty gross—there could be as much as a pint of thick, greenish, smelly juice in it. My job was to go to the front, lance the abscess, and flush it out. I've done it a thousand times. It stinks a bit, and sometimes the cow slings her head when you lance it, so it sprays everything within fifteen feet or so.

This lump must have had some pretty good pressure because it flew in every direction. It triggered a reaction not commonly displayed by cow folk. A deep, building retching sound began all around me.

As it happened, the two day-worker dudes had weak stomachs when it came to lumpy jaw juice.

That, coupled with a few too many beers the night before, led to a rather unseemly symphony. But they weren't alone. The ranch owner was doubled over, too, which was unusual behavior, from my experiences with him. It turned out that the only thing that makes him vomit is watching someone else go first.

But his noises were a bit different. He would retch a second, then laugh a second...retch a second and then laugh a second. This, of course, made me laugh. Soon, everyone around was laughing except the two day workers, who were not amused at all.

I guess it surprised me to realize that even these two hard-core dudes had a weak spot. They got better in a few minutes, and we went right back to working cattle as though the spontaneous symphony had never happened.

# Moment 4

### Teeth and Marshal

We always seem to have an eye on teeth. Many of our patients would like to sink them into us. Today, though, the kind of teeth we were watching out for was a bit unusual.

Dr. Zach Smith was knee-deep in stink. The mare was pregnant, but the baby had died inside of her several days before she arrived at the clinic. You can just imagine what this must have been like—bare bones with decomposing flesh attached. This makes for a smell that you just can't know until you've experienced it.

As is usually the case, several people were standing around watching and willing to lend a helping hand. It is a slow and tortuous job. The fly population was having a heyday. They were buzzing and landing on everything.

The crowd started thinning as the really smelly parts started coming out. Only the dedicated and brave at heart remained. One gentleman, in particular, was determined not to let Zach go it alone. He was gloved up and bouncing from place to place like a puppy dog around the table, just waiting for his chance to jump in and help.

The parts became bigger and bigger until finally the torso started its journey out. The smell became overwhelming. It was at about this time that the gentleman (we'll call him Mr. Teeth) got a nose full of the wretched stink. This is one of those smells that is so bad that you can perceive it with organs other than just your nose. It seems to get into your eyes, the pores of your skin, and the hair in your nostrils, and it even has a taste. It was noticeable that Mr. Teeth was getting all of his senses saturated as the large part of the foal came sliding out.

Turns out this fellow had just gotten false teeth. I guess the smell had saturated these new chompers. Whatever the case, it started some of those gut-busting heaves. They started slow and silent. Then they developed into longer, louder contractions of the chest and stomach. All attention left the horse and went to Mr. Teeth.

"Run away! He's gonna blow!" yelled Zach as the crowd started backing away.

Mr. Teeth was making all kinds of guttural noises now. His cheeks would puff out like Louis Armstrong's, only to be followed by a deep puffing sound as his dry lips succumbed to the building pressure of each dry heave. He was running around in circles, looking for a place to spew. The situation was further complicated by the nasty gloves he was wearing. Each time he would reach toward his face to quiet the swells, the goo that was on the gloves would increase the intensity of the smell.

People were scattering like buckshot, but they all wanted to stay close enough to see what happened next.

Zach started barking orders. "Puke in the sawdust! Don't run that way; there's nothing to vomit on! Go outside! Take your gloves off!"

None of the words seemed to penetrate the prevomit fog that had overtaken Mr. Teeth. He just kept running in circles and touching his face with the slimy gloves. It seemed like it was going to go on forever.

It was on about his thirtieth small lap that the sound of those teeth chattering became the dominant noise. They were bumping into his lips, his gums, and each other. It sounded a bit like somebody rolling dice in a Yahtzee cup. It was obvious that everyone was ready to duck when those babies came flying out. It was just a question of which way they were going to go; as he would spin, the audience would bend and rise at the waist like football fans doing the Wave.

Finally, they left through his lips. There was enough pressure built up by now to propel them at a rapid rate. Mr. Teeth had managed to slip behind the surgery room, into an area that afforded a safe launch. No one actually saw it happen. The noise was something similar to a car backfiring, followed by a high-pitched ping as the teeth flew out of his mouth and bounced off a metal I beam.

Ghastly looks were immediately replaced by high eyebrows and gut-busting laughter. After finishing the job, Mr. Teeth calmly went over, picked up the new teeth, and simply put them back in his mouth. What a day.

*seventeen*

# Oddballs

# Moment 1

### Tough Guy

I can spin around one time on one of those carnival rides, and that's it; I'll be sick. Don't ask me why, but it just makes me sick. When I was a kid, I could ride them all day without a problem. Not anymore.

So, I can understand when people come to the clinic and get sick. Thank goodness, gross smells and sights don't bother me at all. We see some of the grossest things imaginable at the clinic. No matter how bad it gets, it has yet to make me pass out or vomit. I have to admit, I have come close a couple of times, but it has never actually happened.

It was a fairly cold night a few Novembers ago. Some high school kids from a neighboring town had been waiting for a couple of hours for a hernia surgery on a show pig.

The owner of the pig was a macho eighteen-year-old who had aspirations of being a veterinarian.

He had been prancing around the clinic telling everyone that someday he was going to be the greatest veterinary surgeon of the twentieth century.

I was ignoring him. It is fairly common to have a preveterinary person in the crowd. I like to let the kids with 4-H projects glove up and help with the surgeries on their animals. Of course, "He-Man" jumped at the chance to be involved.

We scrubbed him up and showed him how to put on the gloves. But, before any of this could occur, he had to take a dip of snuff. This is a required practice for all pubescent he-men these days.

And this was not your run-of-the-mill dip of snuff, either. This kid must have shoved half a can of Copenhagen in his mouth. He just kept packing snuff into the space between his bottom lip and gum. I would not have believed that much snuff could fit in one space.

When he had finished packing and pushing, his face had taken on a distorted, almost deformed, shape. I was amazed and told him so. Anyway, the attention seemed pleasing to him, and he went on.

The surgery consists simply of cutting the skin over the area where a pig's belly button would be and closing the rent in the muscle. Then the skin is reapposed, and the surgery is over. No big deal. I've done it a hundred times.

I explained to He-Man what was about to happen and told him not to touch anything with the sterile gloves he was wearing unless I told him to. I also told him to keep his hands above his elbows. This keeps anything from falling or dripping onto the sterile gloves.

Now get this picture in your mind.

Here stands He-Man. His bottom lip is sticking out like a diving board over a pool. He is holding his sterile hands over this head and trying not to touch anything unless he is told to do so. He has turned his cap around backward and is strutting around for all the other students.

He was really beginning to get on my nerves. It was late and cold, and I was ready to go home.

"On with the surgery," he boasted, "the future of veterinary surgery has arrived." He was quite a show-off.

I made the skin incision. There was very little bleeding. After this, I dissected through the tissue until I reached the hernial sack, and then I cut it. In these procedures, I usually let the kid feel around and become familiar with the anatomy and then show him how to suture up the skin.

This is exactly what I intended for this surgery. I was into the hernial sack. When this is cut, the intestines are exposed. I was about to get He-Man to stick his fingers into the hernia so he could get a feel for what had happened.

I suddenly noticed a clump of brown substance fall from the sky, into the surgery field.

I hate it when something nonsterile enters a surgical field. I looked up to see what in the world had come from the ceiling of the clinic.

When my glance returned to the surgical field, another clump of stuff bounced off the drape. I was puzzled.

I looked over at He-Man to see if he knew where it was coming from. It was at this moment that I realized what had happened.

He-Man didn't look too good. He was white as a sheet and looked like a boxer after he stood up from a nine-count. The brown stuff was not falling from the ceiling, but from his bottom lip.

Not only snuff, but a steady stream of slobber was rolling down his chin. Through all the delirium, he had not put his hands down. He was beginning to look dizzy. Still, hands were up. I yelled for someone to catch him just as he started down. Two people standing next to him softened his blow.

Now, he was lying on his side on the concrete with his hands still above his head and snuff all over the inside of his mouth and the floor around him. His hat was down around his eyes. We could not stop the surgery to tend to him. There is only a finite amount of time that the anesthesia will be in effect.

Strangely enough, no one seemed to care that He-Man was down. They just stepped over him and finished watching the surgery.

In a minute, he began to stir. It must have been a strange feeling to wake up on the floor of a veterinary clinic with your hands gloved and above your head, not knowing where you were or how you got there. The first noise he made was a gurgle. This was followed by some crazy words that could not be understood.

The words were followed by the noise that means, "I have too much snuff in my stomach, and it is going to have to come out very soon."

His pig did well. The other kids there had a big time. I'm almost sure his career choice changed. But I know he was a very humble He-Man on his trip home.

# Moment 2

### *Hippie*

The foal was in bad shape when it arrived from three hours away. It was colicked, and all the tests looked bad. As if that wasn't enough reason to be bummed out, the owners were oddballs. The woman was a registered hippie, and her boyfriend was wearing a do-rag with a sports jacket and cutoff jeans. And to top that off, they were anal-retentive about the foal, asking questions so fast I didn't have time to answer the first before they started asking the second.

I can deal with badly colicked foals, but crazy owners who won't quit asking questions and worry about tiny details drive me nuts. After dealing with them for twenty-two years, I have lost all ability to cope with them. These people may have been the worst I have ever seen. They wanted to stand in the surgery room while the surgery was going on. I politely told them that there was a big window that looked into the horse surgery room, and they could watch through that.

I informed the veterinarian running anesthesia that I did not want this foal getting too deep. There are many valid scientific reasons to keep foals in this condition from getting overanesthetized, and I had a serious look on my face as we entered surgery and I told her this. She followed my instructions to a T. There were several times during the surgery that the foal became a little light, but I was not complaining because I did not want its blood pressure or cardiac output compromised.

The surgery went well. We found the problem and corrected it in short order. I told the crew, as I left it with them to close the incision, that I did not want this critter dying from anesthesia.

The foal's owners greeted me outside the surgery room in front of the window with over a thousand questions, just as I expected. The hippie woman was now mad at the do-rag-wearing boyfriend because he was asking questions faster than she was, and I just stood there watching them argue over whose turn it was to ramble meaningless questions that had no answer.

As luck would have it, they were standing with their backs to the window, and I was facing them. I noticed all the people in the surgery room suddenly begin moving quickly with deliberate intent. I noticed that the foal was moving on the table. It was waking up before they had time to get it off the table, which was good in a way and bad in a way. Good because it was not going to die from the effects of the anesthesia; bad because if these people turned around and saw that baby moving on the table, they were gonna prolapse.

All of the people in the surgery room were looking with big eyes at me. I could tell they all realized that if the hippie and do-rag dude ever turned around and saw even a glimpse of this, they were gonna have a come-apart. Somehow, I never changed expressions. Don't ask me how; I usually have no poker face at all. I even managed to use only my peripheral vision to assess the situation. I never lost eye contact with the bickering duo.

Then they began to turn their bodies to a position that might allow the motion in the surgery room to grab their attention. This made me go into action.

Instead of listening to their questions, I began to volley a continuous stream of meaningless questions their way. While rattling off these questions, I got louder, more serious, and gradually moved to my right, which made them turn their backs to the window once again. I wouldn't even let them finish answering a question before I bellered out the next one with even more conviction in my voice and jacked my eyebrows higher on my forehead. This seemed to be just what they longed for. They were hypnotized by my tone and facial expressions. They were digging deep into their gray matter for equally explosive answers.

This went on for a good five minutes, until the surgery crew could get the foal into the recovery room. When the door shut to that room, my face immediately went back to an expressionless skin bag with many eye wrinkles. They seemed to be disappointed by the subliminal interaction that had just occurred. In fact, they both paused for a moment and looked into the now-empty surgery room.

"Wow, we were so involved in the conversation, I didn't even see them take our foal out of the room. I sure hope she wakes up soon. It is the scariest part of surgery, you know."

I could hear laughter coming from the lab that adjoins the exam room in which I was talking to these people. I knew what they were laughing about, even though I couldn't make out a word they were saying. I eventually sent the people on their way and got to rehash the entire event from the other side of the window. The crew was more proud of me for managing to keep those people from seeing the pandemonium than for anything I have done before or since.

I love this job.

# Moment 3

## *Mouse Man*

As a veterinarian, you just never know what you are going to do each day.

This was a day not unlike many others around the clinic. We had a busy morning, and the afternoon was shaping up to be just another day when our receptionist, Berenda, told me that I had a phone call. She said it must be one of my college buddies playing a joke on me. I answered the phone as I usually do and then just sat in the chair listening, as my mouth fell wider and wider open with amazement.

It seemed that the caller had a pet mouse with a tumor on it. This person was calling from a good ways away and wanted to drive to my clinic in Lamesa to have this mouse's tumor removed. Upon further questioning, it turned out that this individual had several pet mice, about a hundred or so. But the history was not over. This person now informed me that he had no money and wondered if I would remove the tumor from Rosey for free. This person said that he had already tried to "strangulate" the tumor on the mouse by tying some carpet thread around it, but it didn't work. When asked how big the tumor was, I was surprised to learn it was bigger than the mouse!

So, if you were in my shoes, what would you have said? What would you have done? Would you have said, "Come on in?" Would you have thought it was a college buddy and just hung up? I had never done a surgery on a mouse. I wasn't even sure how to sedate one in order to do surgery!

Well, for some unknown reason, I said, "Sure, come on in."

I halfway thought that no one would ever show up. I figured some-one was messing with me and when I hung up, he would call back and say, "Gotcha!"

But that never happened. In fact, about an hour later, he showed up. It was not a joke.

Sitting in the waiting room of the clinic was this person with a one-ounce mouse that had a four-ounce tumor. The tumor was so large the mouse couldn't even carry it around. It was on the mouse's head. The tumor looked like the Michelin Man. It was white and undulating. You could see where the attempted strangulation with carpet thread had occurred. Other than having this mammoth growth, the mouse seemed just fine. The person told me that it ate, drank, and went to the bath-room normally.

With that in mind, we set about the task of figuring out how to anes-thetize this critter. We decided the best and least dangerous way would be to just put the entire mouse in a mask that we use to gas down large dogs. We sorta made a miniature gas chamber. Manda, my technician, held her hand over the hole, and we turned the gas on. It worked like a charm. This mouse was now in the perfect state for a good, old-fashion tumor removal.

It takes some tiny instruments to work on a mouse. We used eye-surgery instruments. The surgery was going along just great, when all of the sudden, I heard the extreme "Oh no" gasp from Berenda and Manda. It is the kind of noise that makes you stop everything you are doing and take notice.

I looked down at what they were pointing at, and there it was. It looked as if the mouse had developed a rectal prolapse. So, now I am thinking, *How am I going to fix a prolapse on a one-ounce mouse? It is hard enough to fix one on a thousand-pound cow!*

So here's the situation: I've got this person sitting out in the wait-ing room who is becoming more and more hysterical as each moment passes. I can hear him crying and talking to himself. Now I have a pro-lapsed mouse on the table and no idea of how to repair it. I'm 50 per-cent finished removing this mouse from the tumor, and it is bleeding profusely.

It was almost to the point of complete and utter hopelessness. I decided that I had to finish the tumor surgery, and then I would worry about the prolapse. The bleeding was too extreme to stop now. So, I set about finishing the removal. It was going well. I was trying to make the thing as cosmetically pleasing as possible.

We were just about to finish the tumor removal when the prolapse starting moving. That's right. It was moving and squirming. It was then we realized that the mouse was not prolapsed, and it was not a boy. The stress of tumor removal had thrown this gal into labor. She was having a baby. I was tremendously relieved not to have to fix a prolapse.

We finished the surgery and sent the mouse home to finish her delivery. The man was more than happy. He actually gave me all the money he had on him (a dollar) and continually thanked me as he walked out the door. As far as I know, the mouse is fine and still having herds of cancer-prone babies.

# Moment 4

### Tooth Lady

As a consultant veterinarian at a feed yard, you entrust the health program of thousands of cattle to a group of people who are referred to as "doctors." They are not really doctors; that is just the term used by the people who work at the yard to describe what they do. It is the consultant's job to train these people to treat sick cattle, and it can be a frustrating task. Here is an example of why.

Dan Thompson and I arrived at the feed yard at around 6:00 a.m. This particular feed yard used two young women as the doctoring crew. They were not the brightest of individuals, which makes the task of teaching them complicated "doctoring" terms even more difficult. You might wonder why I say they were not too bright. Well, here is why.

One of the girls was sitting on a table with a twisted look on her face. The expression seemed to reflect a mixture of disgust and pain. I couldn't really tell which, so I approached and began asking questions.

It seemed that her boy, Junior, was having problems in school. In fact, they had put him back to the third grade, and considering that it was February, this must have been significant.

"He's not a dummy. I'm telling you, those stupid teachers just don't know how to teach someone with an IQ as high as his. My momma told me that Junior is just so smart that he gets bored with the slow pace they set over at the elementary school," were the words that came rolling out of the side of her mouth as she began describing the unfortunate events of the last few days.

The expression on her face just didn't seem to match the emotion that should have come with the "stupid" people over at the elementary school. No, it was something more...something almost painful. Suddenly she reached up and cupped her chin with both hands. A mild moan trickled from that same corner of her mouth, and she winced a bit.

"Besides all that, I have a toothache, and it is killing me!"

Dr. Thompson quickly chimed in. "Well, why don't you go to the dentist?"

"I hate dentists. They scare me, and they are all stupid. It got to hurtin' so bad last night that I just pulled it myself."

"You mean to tell me that you pulled your own tooth?" Dr. Thompson squealed, his eyebrows began to get higher on his forehead. "How did you do that?"

"I just got a pair of vise grips and started wiggling it. It must have tooken about an hour of serious wiggling before I got it out. I even had to get my husband to hold my head down because my neck got tired."

"You've got to be kidding. You mean you actually pulled your own *tooth*?" Dan asked as the anticipation of what happened next began to build. He went on to request an examination of the area that the tooth once occupied. Sure enough, there was a giant gap about two or three teeth back on the upper left arcade.

"How come it still hurts so bad if you pulled it out?" Dan asked.

"Well...I pulled the wrong one. Turns out the one that really hurts is the next one back."

So, you tell me: how far did the apple fall from the tree? How would you like to entrust the healthcare of millions of dollars' worth of cattle to this gal? Furthermore, how would you like to be responsible for teaching her?

# Moment 5

### Pigs at a Football Game

Friday nights in the fall can mean only one thing—high school football. All over America, fans flock on cool evenings to cheer for their boys as the "pigskin" is passed, kicked, and handed off. This Friday night was no different, except, perhaps, for the type of pigskin that was involved.

The phone rang about three o'clock. It was a concerned pig owner. It sounded as if one of his prizewinning show hogs had developed a cyst after a recent castration. His voice was filled with the tone of "too many things to do" as he described how hopelessly cluttered his schedule was for the next few days.

"Do you reckon you could meet me at the football game tonight and fix that pig for me?" was the question he posed.

The silence hung as I contemplated the request.

"I figure that the stadium is about halfway between us, and I sure would appreciate it if you could help me out here," he said.

A sarcastic "great" was the first thing to enter my mind in the seconds that passed as I formulated an answer for this request. How was I going to do surgery on a pig, in the dark, at a six-man football game? It was freezing cold, and besides, I had already made plans with the family for this evening. My mind was telling me this was a dumb idea, but duty called, and I kinda felt sorry for this fellow after hearing the sob story that preceded the farfetched request.

It was eight o'clock and pitch-black when I arrived at the football field. Six-man football in West Texas can be very competitive or an absolute blowout. When you have only forty-two kids in the entire high school, it is sometimes hard to round up even six boys who want to play football.

The scoreboard read twenty-eight to nothing in the second quarter. The stands were sparsely filled with a few heavily clothed fans who, I could tell, were blowing frost with each exhale as I pulled up to the visiting team's end zone. There, parked under the last set of lights illuminating the field, was the trailer filled with my mission. I was amazed that this guy had parked a trailer in the end zone of a football game and even more amazed that no one had asked him to move it. But in these little football fields, it is kinda hard to tell where the parking lot ends and the football field begins.

"I figured that was the best light in the county," he said. "If you need some help, just holler. We'll be setting right over there. Our boy is playing quarterback tonight, and we don't want to miss a play. Oh, by the way, some of our neighbors threw in a few more pigs that just need castrating."

Here is the situation: I am about to work on a trailer full of pigs, by myself, on a freezing Friday night, in the end zone of a six-man football game. To make matters worse, the pigs weigh about 120 pounds apiece.

The "great" that had filled my mind earlier now had gone from sarcastic to disgusted.

I gathered all the tools needed for such an undertaking and entered the trailer. It didn't take long for the squealing and fighting to get started. I entered the back compartment of the trailer first and determined to finish this bunch before I went to the front compartment. They screamed and rocked the trailer as each injection of sedative went in.

Ten minutes later, I was done and ready to go on to the critters in the front. As I opened the gate leading deeper into the trailer, I realized that there was just one pig there. He was a monster. Hanging out of his back end was an infected "cord" that was just begging to be cut off. I sure hated to have to sedate such a large pig on this freezing night simply to snip off a little cord that had swollen. I contemplated my options carefully and decided it would be safer for the pig if I just snared his nose and snipped the cord off. It would take just a second and would be painless, almost like giving a Band-Aid a quick jerk instead of slowly pulling it off.

I set about snaring the critter. We bounced off every wall of that trailer as I missed time and time again. That rascal had obviously been snared before and didn't like it a bit. The more I tried and missed, the more determined I became to catch him. The trailer rocked, and the pig screamed. Finally, after what seemed like five minutes, I captured the monster. I was covered with pig excrement as I secured the screaming pig to the trailer. It took less than a second to remove the cyst, and I set the pig free. My ears were ringing from five minutes of noise that rivaled a 747 taking off. My shoulder was aching from being bounced off the walls and stepped on a few times. Nevertheless, the fact that it was finally over quelled the discomfort as I headed for the back gate to make my exit.

As I stepped out into the light of the end zone and brushed myself off, I couldn't help but notice how quiet it was. I was beginning to think that the game was over and everyone had left, when a thunderous cheer met me. They had stopped the game, and the referee was standing on the five-yard line looking with concerned eyes at me. Both stands were cheering for me, as they evidently had found more entertainment in screaming pigs in a rocking trailer than in the lopsided game. The players were behind the ref, clapping along with the fans.

As I drove home, I couldn't help but think that nowhere but in rural America could you stop a football game for a pig castration.

# Moment 6

## Do They Really Make Them That Big?

One of the fringe benefits of working at a veterinary clinic is an occasional bit of entertainment. That's because animals can be just plain funny at times. You never really know what they'll do next. It puts some fun into our lives and is one of the reasons we veterinarians have the best job in the world.

The dog, a German shepherd mix, checked into the Brock Veterinary Clinic motel on a Wednesday to board with us over Thanksgiving and for a few days after.

The animal ate, drank, barked, played, and spent the days just like all the other kennel residents. Nothing about the dog provided a clue of what was going to happen on Monday afternoon.

All was normal that day until about 1:00 p.m., when something in the German shepherd's cage caught technician Laura's eye. The dog apparently had taken ill and was vomiting.

This was a big deal. We don't like to see our boarders getting sick, so Laura hurried back to investigate.

What she found made her come running into the clinic to get the rest of us.

She was blushing.

She announced that the German shepherd had coughed up something in his cage, and we all needed to come have a look.

I couldn't imagine what a dog would disgorge that would make her face turn red, but I was about to find out.

On the way, I wondered what the animal might have ingested; it had to be something he swallowed during his stay with us. Whatever it was, it had put the strangest look on Laura's face.

Have I done a good enough job of building up the suspense?

I'll give you a hint: it was red.

We rounded the corner and could see the dog looking through the cage door, as happy and content as could be. No sign of depression or any other indication that he didn't feel well. In fact, by this time, he was wagging his tail and seemed excited to see us. I couldn't wait to see what had caused the commotion.

Then, there it was: a red thong pantie—just lying there after having spent five days in the belly of the whale.

How could this be? There wasn't a tooth mark on it.

This dog must have swallowed the thong whole. It had been in his stomach for five days, and then his system rejected it just a few hours before he was scheduled to go home.

Wow.

I've seen dogs bring up that red rind around a slice of bologna, toy soldiers, milk cartons, paper towels, watermelon seeds, candy-bar wrappers, ponytail holders, nuts, bolts, and an entire cat.

But I never would have believed that a dog could, or would, swallow a red thong pantie, hold it in his stomach for five days, and then toss it up in mint condition.

I couldn't decide whether I should tell the owner when she came to pick up her dog.

We decided just to put the item a plastic bag and ask if she wanted it back.

She, of course, did not.

# Moment 7

*Motorcycles*

This episode begins at 2:00 a.m. in an old Chevy pickup as I headed to sew up a horse. It was going to take another hour or so of driving, according to the directions I had received over the phone from the frantic woman.

*Wonder why they couldn't get a vet a little closer than me to come out?* I pondered. *No one else is stupid enough to answer the phone...Maybe all the vets in that area know these people, and there is something wrong with them...Man, is it cold...I won't get back home until four or five in the morning...*

As I arrived at the location, I began to think that I must have written down the directions wrong. I was pulling into what appeared to be a junkyard. Car skeletons lined an area that was illuminated by one old streetlight.

I pulled in slowly to be met by the silhouettes of rows of Harley motorcycles. Just as I was about to turn around and leave, a figure appeared out of the shadows of an old tin building.

He was a very large man. He was wearing a helmet with a metal spike coming out of the top, a pair of tattered jeans, and a leather vest. It must have been forty degrees outside, and this guy was wearing nothing but a sleeveless leather vest. As he got closer, I could see that he was covered with tattoos. Before he reached the window of my pickup, more figures began to appear.

I was a little panicked. It was three o'clock in the morning, and I was in a junkyard with a motorcycle gang. What were the odds that these people had a horse? How was I going to explain to these folks why I had invaded their turf?

"You the vet doctor?" were the first words that hit my ears. They came in a very gruff tone that seemed to echo off all the dead cars that surrounded us. "My horse got a bad cut on his belly. Come on in."

I couldn't believe it! These people actually had a horse! He pointed toward the tin barn and motioned for me to follow him. I pulled the truck closer and timidly exited with my vet bag. Inside were thirty or so leather-clad individuals and one cut-up horse. The room was totally silent as I entered. I could feel their eyes inspecting me as I ambled over to examine the horse.

The spokesman for the group was the giant man's girlfriend, who was dressed just like he was. She began to explain to me how the horse cut himself, but I was so taken by the entire scene that I barely heard a word she said. The horse had a huge laceration that ran across just in front of his front legs. A large flap of skin about the size of a paper grocery sack hung down under the belly area. This was amazing, but it was nothing compared with the man who was holding the horse. He had on sunglasses and was wearing a pair of leather earmuffs that covered only one ear. On the top of the other ear, between his head and the sunglasses, was one of those two-sided razor blades like my dad used to shave with. This razor blade just stayed there, as though it was embedded in the top of his ear.

As if all of this was not bad enough, I knew I was going to have to sedate this horse in order to suture the monstrous wound. What were these people going to do when they saw what this sedative did to the horse? I'm thinking fast, now. The last thing I wanted was to be mugged for my horse sedative. I could just see these folks experimenting with the effects of horse tranquilizers.

I pulled out the sedative and drew it into the 12-cc syringe. As I was pulling it up, the one with the razor blade on his ear said, "Hey, doctor dude, whatcha got in the syringe?"

"This is Rompun. It's a horse tranquilizer," bubbled out of my lips with a pubescent tone.

"Cool. What'll it do to people?" he gruffed back at me.

"Well, due to the greater vascularity of the human brain, this stuff will almost always cause a stroke-like seizure if it is taken by people." That was probably the biggest line of bull in the world.

"Harsh," was all he had to say.

Now, for the next problem. How was I going to fix this horse? I have felt pressure to fix animals many times in my career, but never like this. I was pretty sure that these people were not going to accept anything less than a perfect horse when I finished.

It took me close to two hours to suture this rascal. I put more stitches in that horse than any other animal in my career—not because it was the biggest cut I've ever sewed, but because I really didn't want to ever see these people again in my life.

After more than an hour of driving, two hours of sewing in a barn at a junkyard, being surrounded by people who looked like they needed to be in a Clint Eastwood movie—and all this done in near darkness—the tattooed lady handed me a sticky note with an address scribbled on it, while the giant man told me to send him a bill.

All I could think of was, *Fine with me. If I leave this place alive, I don't care if I ever get paid.*

About a month later, we got a letter in the mail. It was from the gang. They were just writing to tell me thanks for fixing the horse. He was doing great. They had taken out the stitches themselves (I guess with the razor blade on the horse holder's head), and they were very thankful that I had come out in the middle of the night. Also enclosed was a check for the full amount.

# Moment 8

*Tattoos*

Tattoos have become quite popular these days. At Texas Tech, where I teach, about one student in three sports some kind of artwork.

But what do you think the folks at the tattoo parlor would say if you asked them to tattoo a pig?

The pig I'm referring to was supposed to have a dark-colored nose with a red overtone. In any case, it wasn't supposed to be pink. The owner had put the piglet next to a heat lamp that was too close to the ground, and it burned a large spot on the end of the animal's nose.

The spot turned pink as the pig grew. But pink just isn't acceptable in the pig-show world.

My task was to tattoo the nose with something that would restore the correct color.

Just to be clear: I am not a tattoo artist. I don't have anything that even resembles a tattoo instrument. I told the owner he'd have to call a tattoo artist because I had no way of doing it (and really didn't want to be seen tattooing a pig's nose, anyway).

He asked if I would sedate the pig if he found someone to do the job, stating that the pig was going to get a nose tattoo one way or another and that he'd prefer it be sedated for the procedure.

He borrowed our telephone directory and pulled out his cell phone. I listened as he explained the situation to several tattoo artists in the area. Most hung up or laughed so loud I could hear them through the receiver from across the room.

So, no one was willing to tattoo a pig's nose? Go figure.

But three days later, the owner called to say he'd found the right tattoo artist. He made an appointment to bring in the pig for sedation and tattooing.

I was mortified. What kind of guy would tattoo a pig's nose? And who would want to be tattooed with that machine after it poked holes in a hog's schnoz?

My answer came about four hours later when the owner showed up with the pig. Sure enough, it did have a quarter-sized discoloration on the end of the nose. Obviously, it was a very good pig except for that burned spot.

About ten minutes later, the tattoo dude arrived.

"Holy mackerel!" was all I could say to myself as this fellow came ambling across the parking lot with a briefcase full of tattooing supplies. He stood about six seven, must have weighed three hundred pounds, and his entire exposed surface was covered with tattoos.

The pig needed castrating, so I sedated it and quickly removed the testicles. With my job completed, I stepped back and watched as this giant man began unpacking his arsenal of tattoo gear. He explained that he had built the tattoo gun from a VCR motor and that it was the most powerful one around—just right for a hog's nose.

His next move made our jaws drop. He pulled off one boot and sock, exposing the top of his foot, on which he had tattooed about twenty thin lines of various shades of reddish-brown. The tattoos looked fresh, still red and irritated on the edges. He then held the foot next the sedated pig's nose and asked which shade best matched the nose's natural color.

"Dude, did you tattoo those lines on your foot just for this?" I asked incredulously.

"Yep. When I saw that hog on Monday, I realized I would never be able to match the color if I didn't have som'in' to compare it to," he replied.

So there we stood, maybe seven people at varying distances, trying to decide which color line on the man's foot most closely matched the pig's nose.

Picture it: This giant man is holding his foot three feet off the ground next to the nose of a sedated pig. He moves it back and forth so that each line briefly touches the nose for accurate comparison.

After a great deal of debate, we decided on a color, and he went to work.

It took him about fifteen minutes. The result was smashing. You couldn't tell the slightest difference between the color of the normal nose and the tattoo.

The thrilled owner pulled out his wallet and gave the guy forty dollars.

Forty dollars? I charged the owner more than that to sedate the pig and castrate it.

That guy tattooed his own foot and then a pig's nose for forty dollars?

I don't know what I was expecting. I guess I was just going on what I would have charged someone to tattoo my foot and then the nose of a pig.

You can bet it would be somewhere in the six-figure range.

# Moment 9

*Meatballs*

"Hey, Doc, I got a question for ya. I ate some dog medicine, and I just need to know if it is gonna kill me."

These were the words I was greeted with first thing as I rolled into the parking lot of the clinic at seven o'clock Wednesday morning. And coming from Butchee, those words could do nothing except evoke wonderment and make me laugh.

But he had no humorous expression on his face. In fact, his face was twisted up a bit with worry.

Butchee is a big fella. I don't mean fat or outta-shape kinda big, either. He is just a big man. He is gettin' close to fifty and is a hardworking farmer around here. I have known him for twenty years. He has a dog named Gator that makes every mile and every moment with him. Gator is a big yellow Lab that is getting a little old.

Butchee's wife had brought Gator into the clinic on Monday, and Dr. Dustin McElwee had dispensed some NSAIDs for ol' Gator to combat the aches and pains that come from running around as a farm dog for nine years. Dustin told her to put the pill in a piece of cheese or a meatball, and Gator would just eat it up.

Mrs. Butchee got home that Monday evening and was delighted to find that a few of the meatballs she had prepared for Sunday dinner were still in the fridge. Perfect. Dustin said meatball, and she just happened to have seven left. It appeared that she now had a vehicle for an entire week's worth of Gator's pain pills.

Mrs. Butchee took one of the meatballs out and poked a pill into it. She was about to take it outside to Gator when the phone rang. It was a call from her mother, who needed immediate help with something. So Mrs. Butchee drove over to Mom's, leaving the one spiked meatball and six normal meatballs setting on the counter.

A little while later, Butchee arrived home after a hard day's work and saw seven meatballs just begging to be eaten. He slurped them all down and went on about his evening.

When Mrs. Butchee arrived back home, she had forgotten all about the dog pain pills and the meatballs. And since Butchee actually cleaned up the mess, there was nothing to remind her.

"Let me tell you som'in', Doc. Them pain pills you gave Gator work! I ran around the farm yesterday like a little kid. I was jumping over fences, and my back felt better than it has in years. I couldn't figure out why I felt so good. I felt so good yesterday that I just up and challenged Deaver—a twenty-year-old college boy—to an arm-wrestling match at the gin and whipped him.

"Yeah, I ate that pill," Butchee said, "and the missus forgot all about them pills until this morning, when she remembered Doc Dustin had given them to her. She looked high and low for those meatballs and then asked me if I had seen them. When I told her I ate them all, she just started laughing and asked me if one of them tasted funny. You reckon that pill gonna have any bad effects on me?"

I could tell this was a trick question. If I told Butchee that the pill wasn't gonna hurt him, he was gonna take the rest of them and forget about ol' Gator. There was too much conviction in his description of how good he felt all day Tuesday for me to believe that dog would ever get another pill.

I decided to use farmer logic. I raised one eyebrow and replied, "Have you had the urge to hike your leg when you pee? Have you felt like lapping up water with just the use of your tongue? Do you feel like you would rather ride in the bed of the pickup than the cab?"

He kinda got a faraway, thoughtful look on his face and replied, "Nope."

"Well then, I guess you didn't get enough in that one pill, but if you take any more of them, you might start feeling those symptoms." I kept an extremely straight face and left that one, hiked eyebrow hanging.

"Are you kidding with me, Doc? Is that why they are dog pills? You mean to tell me that if I woulda took another one today, I might start acting like a dog? I guess they are *dog* pills. Good thing I talked to you. I felt so good yesterday, I started to take another one. Dang."

I don't know if he believed me or not. He kept looking at me to see if he could read any expression on my face that might indicate if I was joking or serious. I do know that Gator got the rest of the pills. And I do know that every time I see Butchee, he wants to know if I was kidding with him or telling the truth.

# Moment 10

### *Good People*

It is no surprise that clients take up as much and usually more time than the animals we treat. Consequently, clients become the topic of many conversations, both inside and outside of the clinic. Most of the time, these conversations revolve around people who made us laugh because they, themselves, were funny or because they were plain idiots, or people who made us furious because they were overly demanding or, again, because they were idiots. Unfortunately, the people who often are left out of the conversations are those who deserve to be in them—clients who display deep devotion and compassion for their animals and respect for the veterinarians' efforts to heal. The following are a couple of the many who deserve recognition and whose tales will, I hope, spark kind thoughts and memories of others.

Angel was a miniature horse that arrived at the clinic for colic surgery with her owner, Sara. Sara was a college student who, in her free time, used Angel as a therapy pony for children with major disabilities. During the surgery, and with a wide smile on her face, Sara regaled us with stories of kids who wouldn't interact with any species, human or otherwise, until Angel entered the picture.

The next morning, Sara arrived at the clinic with her grandfather, who had driven the six hours from Dallas to support his granddaughter. He obviously was a well-educated and very articulate man, with a faint accent that ended up being a combination of an origin in France and a life in Australia.

Sara had to go back to school three hours away, but Grandpa stayed with us an entire week at the clinic. Every one to two hours, he would

take Angel out to graze and walk, regardless of the summer temperature or time of day. He would stop and chat and inform us of Angel's
behavior, asking intelligent questions in his quiet and kind voice, but
always at appropriate times and never in an obnoxious manner. He also
made a point of visiting with other clients who were bringing in critical
cases and kept track of how everyone was getting along.

One evening, Grandpa exclaimed that the "best part of getting old
was helping his grandchildren," and that anyone who went out of her
way to help others like Sara was doing deserved to be supported as best
as possible. He genuinely said that he appreciated all we were doing, but
that if he could help Angel get well by providing attention throughout
the day, then he would stay as long as it took. While he enriched Angel's
life so that she could go back to enriching the lives of others, Grandpa
also enriched ours while we worked around and with him through the
days.

Marcus was a Thoroughbred eventing horse that was also referred for
colic surgery. With too much small intestine involved to resect, but tissue that wasn't nonviable enough to euthanize, we closed him up and
recovered him, although his prognosis was grim. Sarah and her daughter, Olivia, the seventeen-year-old owner, were emotional yet determined. Over the next three weeks, they showed up without fail every
morning at nine and stayed until six in the evening. Lawn chairs were
popped open in front of the stall or pasture, Marcus was meticulously
groomed and loved on, and there was always a bowl of sweet and salty
goodies for us.

The most striking thing about it all was that Olivia arrived petrified of blood and pain. Over the ensuing days, she became my go-to
helper, holding Marcus steady for his new catheters and blood draws,
twitching him while we refluxed, faithfully syringing Well-Gel and Bio-
Sponge, and overcoming her fears for the good of her horse. She trusted
that we were doing what was best. Tears often welled in all of our eyes
as Marcus went on a roller coaster of bad days and good days, fighting

with us as we fought to help him. Ultimately, Marcus succumbed to the fate we feared, but not without creating a strong bond between Sarah and Olivia and all of us at the clinic, which continues on to this day.

For many, being a veterinarian is not a career, but a lifestyle. The hours are not set, the outcomes are rarely certain, and maintaining the line between investing too much emotion or not enough is fine. Angel and Grandpa, the Sara(h)s, and Marcus and Olivia represent those who make our lifestyle as veterinarians worth it at the end of the day. They make the triumphs sweeter; the losses more painful; and they are, without a doubt, worth talking about.

*Section 5*

## Just Stuff

Success in life is simply a ratio of what
we coulda done, to what we did.


Bo Brock
1990

*eighteen*

## Dr. Zach

# Moment 1

### Big Dogs and Zach

On my way home from teaching, I noticed the lights were on at the clinic.

I pulled up to see what was going on and found Dr. Zach Smith gathering up equipment to go on a farm call. It never fails that cows prolapse in the middle of the night.

Listening to Zach describe the situation made me think that this might not be your run-of-the-mill prolapse. In fact, it sounded to me like this might be quite an adventure. I asked if I could tag along, and together we loaded up and headed out to rebuild a cow.

The owner of the cow was gone for a few days, and he had left his wife in charge of the cow herd. As usual, trouble always shows up at the most unwanted times. According to the frantic wife's description, the cow was either "turning inside out" or "giving birth to an elephant, trunk-first."

I guess that would be a good description of a prolapse if you had never seen one before. This woman was not into cows. She was frustrated to have to watch them at all, much less have to chase them into a corral and call out the vet.

We arrived to find a set of very run-down pens sitting in the middle of nowhere. The woman was inside her pickup with the lights shining into a thirty-by-thirty pen. "Dark" did not do justice to how pitch-black it was. He didn't say it, but I knew that Zach and I were thinking the same thing: *How in the world are we going to do this?*

Over years of making farm calls, I have learned to look around before getting out of the truck. Most farms have dogs, and most of these dogs don't like vets and don't like strangers coming into the cow pens.

I noticed them about the time Zach said, "Have a look at the size of them dogs!"

There they were—two big Rottweilers and a weenie dog. They didn't really bark; they just stood by the door of the truck and made throaty growls.

The woman got out of her truck and came to the window of ours. She was trying to describe the situation with the cow when Zach interrupted.

"What about the dogs?"

"They wouldn't bite a biscuit," was her reply, as the pack of them stood next to the window and growled. I wasn't worried about a biscuit. It was veterinarians that concerned me.

She managed to coax us out of the pickup and over to the pens. Zach was doing the talking, and I was pulling up the rear, watching the dogs. In the pen was the entire "herd," one giant bull and three cows. The cow with the prolapse was one of the thinnest animals I had ever seen. Not only that, but she was crippled. So here she stood, four hundred pounds underweight, crippled in one back leg, and prolapsed. What a specimen.

There was no way to restrain the cow. The pen was just a thirty-by-thirty square with a tin roof over one corner.

Zach pulled me aside and asked, "How in the world are we gonna do anything for that cow if we can't catch her?"

"I don't know. Let's just go in and see what happens. Anything would be better than standing out here with these dogs growling at us," I said as we climbed over the fence.

The bull was not a bit happy about intruders. He stood in the corner and pawed the ground. The other two cows started running in circles around the pen. This excited the dogs, and they came through the fence. Now we were standing in the center of the pens, next to the skinny, prolapsed cow, with two wild cows circling, a mad bull, a pair of worked-up Rottweilers, and a weenie dog.

We approached the afflicted cow and began sizing up what we might do. As I got closer, I noticed that she didn't move at all. In fact, I could just walk up and touch her. I was figuring that she would have a hard time kicking with one bad back leg, so I just went to work trying to poke the prolapse back in. She just stood there. Zach was keeping the bull and wild cows off me as I struggled and pushed to put things back together. It was a tough job, like putting a marshmallow in a piggy bank.

With all the straining and sweating, I had forgotten about the pack of dogs. Suddenly, I was surrounded by deep growls. Before I could even react, the dogs grabbed ahold. That's right. They bit down for all they were worth. I was panicked, not because they were biting me; no, it was not me they had sunk their teeth into. It was the cow. One Rottweiler had the tail, one had a back foot, and the weenie dog was running in between the legs, barking and jumping. I was afraid to kick them off the cow because they might just turn on me. I was afraid the cow was going to get a bellyful of it and kick me, trying to get them off. The cow started running. I couldn't quit. The marshmallow was just about back in the piggy bank. I gave a mighty lunge forward just as Zach started hollering at the dogs. The prolapse popped back in, and the dogs scrambled away.

The woman was very impressed. I guess she thought we did stuff like that every day. Her husband got an earful when he got home. I am not sure if he is permitted to leave town ever again.

# Moment 2

*Teamwork*

It is hard to believe that nearly a year has passed since Dr. Smith and his family arrived in Lamesa. They have been a great blessing to the practice and have delivered many new ideas and smiles to the area. We are blessed to have them. The result of working together day after day is that a team spirit develops. This is a good thing that exists between all of us who work here and helps us ride the highs and lows of being together all the time.

I think I remember the moment that Dr. Smith and I developed that team bond. It was another blistering-hot day in August. Nothing unusual about having a few goats at the clinic that time of year. Most of the prospective show goats are having cosmetic dehorns done to get ready for the impending show season. This technique requires heavy sedation. The surgery rivals a dentist standing on your head to remove a wisdom tooth for being the most gruesome procedure known to man.

As is often the case, we were working on four goats for which the owners had paid "way too much" money. The people had driven from about a hundred miles away just to have the cosmetic dehorn performed. They dropped off the goats and left to run a few errands.

Dr. Smith and I went to work to make these creatures look as beautiful as possible. This day was no exception to the usual setting at the clinic. Most of the time, there are a few people standing around either waiting their turns or just watching and asking questions. The first goat was finished and recovering. The recovery usually consists of a gradual wearing off of the sedative, and a slow progression from lying on a side, to lying on the stomach, to standing, to walking with a wobble, to walking, to normal. This process usually takes about two or three hours.

The syringe in my left hand was about to be filled with the medicine in my right hand when I caught a glimpse of movement with my peripheral vision. It must be an instinctive trait in veterinarians, because Dr. Smith noticed it at about the same moment. Having a veterinary clinic next to one of the busiest streets in town has attuned me to the importance of restraining our patients. It took just one two thousand-pound bull running down Dallas Avenue with Wyndell Culp riding behind it on horseback, swinging a rope, to drive this point home.

The series of events that followed seemed to proceed in slow motion for me. My mind was following the events almost as if they were happening to someone else, and I was merely a spectator. The critter made a soft goat sound and then sprang to its feet. Remember, the "spring to the feet and walk normal" part is not supposed to occur for a couple of hours. The garage door beckoned Mr. Goat with the promising light of freedom and reminded Dr. Smith and me that beyond it were no fences.

It may not come to a surprise to you to learn that most animals can outrun a person. It also may not come as a surprise to learn that the human body can do some pretty amazing things when the adrenal glands kick in. I am not certain, but I think it is quite possible that the adrenal glands of the good doctors Smith and Brock completely emptied as that high-dollar goat from a hundred miles off rounded the corner and headed for the open parking lot.

It was truly a team adventure from that point forward. We were keeping up well; Zach on the goat's left side and me on its right. It was one of those moments when I was running so fast that my body was unable to do anything else. I believe the other doctor was feeling the same, because for about a hundred yards, that is all we did. We simply ran along beside; nothing more, nothing less. I was looking at the bottle of medicine and syringe in my hand and thinking, *Throw them down, Bo! Come on, just throw them down.* But I couldn't. I just kept running along beside, looking at the goat with one eye and thinking, *Why can't I throw this needle-bearing syringe down?*

A trailer was approaching at about twelve o'clock. Without any form of communication whatsoever, Dr. Smith and I formulated the exact same plan. We would just stay on either side of the goat, and when he got to the trailer, he would have to stop.

We got to the trailer. The goat stopped.

Dr. Smith continued down the left side of the trailer, and I continued down the right. This left us looking at each other on the other end of the trailer, each of us thinking the other was still back there with the goat. This thought lasted only a second, because the goat was now off again.

Once again, we were off like a flash. This time, the goat was heading for the street. I cannot speak for the thoughts in Zach's head, but I can tell you with painstaking detail all the ones that were racing through mine—first and foremost, change the direction of the goat. I had to do this while carrying a bottle of medicine and a syringe-bearing needle out in front of me because no matter how much I told my hands to drop them, it just wasn't happening. I just accepted this and began to formulate a plan of how I was going to head the goat off with these as a part of my body.

I accelerated with a burst of speed that surprised me—and the goat—but Dr. Smith saw it coming and had backed off just enough to let the goat turn away from me and away from the dangers that the road held. Now we had the goat headed for the neighboring gas station and had a shot at actually grabbing the thing. But how was I going to do any grabbing with my hands full? Not only that, but was I going to be able to do a Johnny Bench slide on my face, chest, and knees? I hadn't done that since the seventh grade.

I knew it was going to take this type of a grab because we could not gain any ground on the goat. We would speed up, and he would too. We would slow down, and he would too. No matter how fast we went, he was going to stay just far enough ahead that we couldn't touch him. Just for a second, I tried running while being bent forward at the waist, thinking that this might close the elusive inches that separated us. I felt myself beginning to fall forward and now was wondering how I was going to break my fall with a bottle of medicine and a syringe in my hands. I was keenly aware at this moment why most professional athletes have retired by my age.

While I was trying to coordinate this offensive capture, Dr. Smith became horizontal. There was a brief, fleeting moment when I saw him fly like Superman over what seemed like twenty yards. His left arm grabbed the back leg of the goat, and I felt relief for the first time in what seemed like a day.

One problem remained. I had to stop, and I had not fully recovered from having my center of gravity too far forward. I went through the eleven basic ballet movements as my feet and legs struggled desperately to get back under my torso. Anyone looking at me during this most ungraceful moment must have been thinking, *Why in the world doesn't he throw down that bottle?*

After a few minutes of high-fiving and hard breathing, it became apparent that we were now officially a team. The goat went home, and the owners never even knew anything happened.

I sat in the coolness of the clinic, holding a bottle of medicine and a syringe, and wondering where my youth had gone.

# Moment 3

### *The Little Red Pig*

The little red pig was in a bad way. His rectum was prolapsed and dragging on the ground. He was limping in both back legs, and he had a mighty cough.

The reason for his visit to the clinic was the least favorite task of a veterinarian—euthanasia.

The owner brought the pig in and gave Dr. Smith the history; he wanted the pig put to sleep. Dr. Smith drew up the correct dose of euthanasia solution and injected it into the vein.

Thirty minutes later, the pig was standing up again.

Dr. Smith took the pig out of the cage so the owner could go home. This time, Zach gave almost twice the dose of euthanasia solution and put the poor red pig in a padded dog cage so he could leave the world in a comfortable setting. Thirty minutes later, he was standing up again.

This was unbelievable. This time, Dr. Smith gave the little red rascal almost three times the prescribed dose of solution. Thirty minutes later, the hog was up and grunting like nothing had ever happened.

Zach suspected that this piggy must be special. He decided to fix the prolapse, treat the pneumonia, and hope the limping got better with time. Daughter number one, Jesslyn, was looking for a 4-H project, and this critter just might be the one.

After getting the OK from the hog's now-previous owner, Dr. Smith set out to repair this strong-willed swine. The treatment was going to be a hard one. It is not easy to fix pneumonia in a pig that size; not to mention a prolapse that was a tremendous mess; not to mention sore joints from a septicemia. It would be a long, uphill battle for this pig to ever even grow, much less be a candidate for the county show.

Father and daughter set about trying to get the little red pig back in shape. The prolapse surgery went well, the pneumonia treatment was progressing with few setbacks, and the limping was improving with each passing day.

"Dr. Dad" soon designed a physical therapy program and strict nutritional plan for the little red pig. Jesslyn went to work, spending most afternoons after school following the plan Dad set out.

By county show time, the miracle pig was looking fine. The months of hard work had saved "Some Pig" from certain death, and he even looked the part of a show pig now. But still, it was Jesslyn's first time to show, and who could ever think that a pig that was nearly dead three times could even have a chance?

Their jaws dropped when the judge proclaimed "Some Pig" was the champion Duroc of the Dawson County show. The Smiths were so sure he didn't have a chance, no one had even thought to bring a camera.

What a story! On Jesslyn's first attempt to show hogs, she took a piggy off of death row, nursed him back from three different ailments (each of which could have been fatal), fed him well enough to catch up with the other pigs that were never even sick, and then beat people who had paid hundreds of dollars for their projects.

Man, what a story!

*nineteen*

## Associates

# Moment 1

*Dr. Deyhle*

The day ended late, and I was just about at the end of my endurance when it occurred to me that I hadn't talked to Dr. Deyhle in quite a while. He was my mentor and took the risk of hiring me straight from veterinary school. He is in his mideighties now, and has been retired about ten years, but he still is quicker-witted than most forty-year-olds.

I had received news a few days earlier that our clinic had earned a practitioner award, and I wanted to give him a call and thank him for getting me off to a good start all those years ago. To this day, I give him credit for instilling an attitude and ethic in me that have persisted.

I was in the middle of thanking him for all he did for me when he interrupted to remind me of an event at the start of my career that I'd rather forget.

After saying he was proud of me and all the things we've been blessed with in Lamesa, he went on to remind me of the first dog I spayed when I went to work with him. I could feel my cheeks turning red as he started recalling the details.

The dog was a big, fat Labrador retriever owned by a decrepit old man who told me it was given to him by his deceased wife. He said the dog meant more to him than anything in the world.

To make matters worse, the dog was in heat. If you are not a seasoned dog spayer, you may not know that there is nothing worse than a big, fat dog in heat. The fat makes everything slick, and the blood vessels are huge and hard to ligate because of the massive amount of encasing tissue.

I had spayed no more than ten dogs in my vet-school career, and none was anything like this one. I was so dumb I didn't even know to be afraid until I cut that rascal open.

Nothing looked like it did in school. Everything was coated with a healthy layer of fat, and I could barely identify anything. One of the key duties of a spay is finding and tying off all the blood vessels that feed the ovaries and uterus. If you don't do that correctly, the dog could bleed to death.

I finally found the artery going to the left ovary and began tying it off. All seemed to be going great until I cut the ovary away and blood squirted all over the room. I could feel my first real case of surgical panic coming on.

"Dr. Deyhle! Dr. Deyhle! You gotta come quick!"

I was about to prolapse. All I could think about was breaking the news to this old fella that his most important possession had passed away.

Meanwhile, where was Dr. Deyhle?

I called out again and again, with no response. I was getting into a frenzy. If something didn't happen pretty quickly, this critter was going to room temperature. I finally took off at a dead run throughout the clinic, looking for him.

Not in his office. Not in the large-animal clinic. Not in the waiting room. Not with the secretaries. Where in the world could he be?

The look on my face must have precluded the need to say anything. The secretary quickly pointed to the bathroom.

Picture this: Just out of school, you're spaying your first dog for a man who has nothing else to live for. You have dropped the stump, and the only person who can save you is...well, indisposed.

Not wanting to break sterility, I began banging on the bathroom door with my elbow, hollering so fast I didn't even understand my own words, but Dr. Deyhle must have picked up on the urgency.

He emerged from the bathroom with his shirt untucked and his pants undone. I will never forget the look on his face—somewhere between panic and embarrassment—as he held up his pants with one hand and fumbled with the bathroom doorknob with the other. He short-stepped down the hall, still holding up his pants.

The tech quickly gloved him, and he went to work fixing everything I'd done wrong. In no time, the bleeding was stopped, and he finished spaying the dog. In fact, he did the entire surgery with his legs apart to keep his pants from dropping. We could find no volunteer to button and zip them while he worked.

"You've come a long way since those days, Bo, but I just want you to know that you will always be a snotty-nosed novice veterinarian to me. That is how you were when I met you, and you had barely passed that stage by the time you left."

I just love that man.

# Moment 2

*Michelle*

Have you ever wondered why the same word used to describe an individual under medical care is also a virtue that requires forbearance and endurance? Do you think that's an accident? I have been practicing veterinary medicine for nearly twenty years, and I can tell you: it's no accident.

Are you a patient person? I'm not. In fact, when Dr. Michelle Dockter recently told me about her experience at a supermarket, it prompted some self-evaluation in me. Here's what happened.

She was in a hurry, as we often are, and the checkout lines were long. She sized them up—looking at the volume of items in people's carts—and finally settled on a line in which customers had just a few items per person.

The old couple just in front of her looked to be retired and had only two things that needed to be purchased. There were a few baskets ahead of the old couple, and the checker working the line was good and fast.

In no time at all, the old couple had laid their items on the counter, and were about to pay, when the old man said, "The newspaper says you have lettuce for sixty-nine cents. We couldn't find any there in the produce section. We want a rain check."

Dr. Michelle was in a hurry to get back to a sick horse. The last thing she needed was to wait for a rain check that saved someone twelve cents on lettuce. To make matters worse, the checker was out of rain checks at her cash register. She started walking from checker to checker, trying to find a rain check to give to these people for sixty-nine-cent lettuce.

No one had a rain check, so the checker had to go to the front office. Dr. Michelle looked around and discovered that she had actually chosen the slowest of all lines and that every customer who would have been behind her in this line was checked out and gone.

Just as she was about to offer the people a dollar if they'd just move on and let her check out, the much-anticipated rain check arrived. But instead of handing the rain check to the elderly couple, the checker started writing on it. It was a generic rain check, and the details about a product had to be filled in and signed by a manager. Of course, there was no manager around, so the checker had to get on the overhead loudspeaker and summon him to her register. Makes you want to pull your hair out just reading about it, doesn't it?

That feeling you're having is a lot like what a dog experiences when it chews its stitches out five minutes after it wakes up from surgery. Or a horse that kicks the stall wall over and over with the leg you spent all day putting a cast on. Maybe a cat that bites and scratches you every time you try to treat it for a disease that will be fatal if it doesn't take the medicine. Or a cow that runs you over and stomps on you while you're trying to deliver the calf that's stuck halfway in and halfway out. With veterinary patients, well, we all just need a little more patience.

# Moment 3

### Stinky Dustin

It had no appointment, but everyone knew it was coming—not by anything other than the smell. When the trailer pulled into the parking lot, over seventy-five yards away, Dr. Dustin McElwee and Dr. Michael Tobias flared their nostrils at the same time and said, "I smell som'in' that is gonna make this evening awful!"

It was Mr. Carter. He is the worst cow client in Dawson County. That rascal never does anything but aggravate veterinarians. It is almost as if it brings him joy to make you either stay late or smell terrible. The only trailer he owns was, perhaps, made for pigs. It is way too short for cattle, but he somehow manages to get a full-grown cow in it.

But getting her out is a different story.

Dr. Dustin saw the trailer and immediately knew where the smell was coming from. Dr. Michael had not met Mr. Carter yet and had no way of knowing why Dustin was grumbling and heading to the clinic to get some coveralls.

After a long episode of near futility, trying to get the cow out of the short trailer, the source of smell became obvious. There were two rotten feet sticking out of the south end of the cow. They were dripping with goo, and the hair was already falling off. The trip through the alleyway to the squeeze chute resulted in the release of gallons of vile liquid, and Dr. Dustin was already trying to decide whether it would be best to burn his clothes or stink up the entire house trying to launder them.

Dr. Michael, the intern, was bouncing around and ready to go. He had never seen Dustin so discouraged over a cow dystocia and was still too new at the clinic to realize what he was about to get into. As is the case with all of Mr. Carter's cows, this one would just as soon kill you as look at you. She fought and snarled all the way to the squeeze chute and then bellered and snorted the entire time they tried to help her.

There was no way that calf was coming out the hole God had put there for it. The thing was rotten. No telling how long she had been in labor, and one slight pull on the leg caused hair, hoof, and skin to just slough off.

"Why you wait so long to bring these things in, Mr. Carter? This cow is gonna die, and the calf is so dead it is decomposing. If you would have just brought her in about three days ago, she might have had a chance," Dr. Dustin proclaimed as he examined the rotting hair in his hand from his first attempt to pull on the calf.

"You can save her, Doc! I got all the faith in the world in ya. Just do a C-section. She will be OK," exclaimed Mr. Carter in a pseudoconfident tone.

There was no need to try to talk him out of it. Dr. Dustin knew that a C-section was going to happen, and that, in the end, everything was going to turn out just terrible. And he was right.

The episode progressed just like a bad dream. Everything that could go wrong, did. The cow strained and fought, kicked and slobbered, and finally (after the abdomen was cut open) lay down. This, of course, meant she was gonna have to be released from the squeeze chute and run back around to be in the right position to pull out the rotting calf.

As she was heading around into the swing-around, her gas-filled rumen sprang through the C-section opening. This is not good. It greatly increases the degree of difficulty of getting a cow through a tight alleyway back into a chute.

Once the critter was finally back into proper restraint, the rumen was decompressed and put back in its home. This left a space to cut the uterus and begin the process of removing a supersmelly fetus. And when that uterus was finally breached, the gust of noxious gas that came pouring forth made everyone gag and tear up.

Dr. Dustin once again told ol' Carter, "This cow is gonna die."

The calf was so dead that rigor mortis had already set in, and it was frozen in position with all legs straight, like a plastic farm animal.

Have you ever tried to remove an unbendable, bloated, hundred-or-so–pound calf from a hole the size of a football? Well, I am here to tell you, it ain't easy.

After about an hour of pulling and tugging, the rotten beast was finally lying on the ground, and as Dr. Dustin stood there panting from exertion, he told Carter, "This cow is gonna die."

They managed to get her back on the trailer after huge doses of pain meds and antibiotics. The last thing Dustin said as Mr. Carter pulled off into the night was, "That cow is gonna die. Don't let her suffer."

Three days later, ol' Carter showed back up at the clinic. He was all crabby and cussing up a storm. Seems the cow died. He was gonna really lay into Dr. Dustin for not saving that cow, but before he could even speak a noun, Dustin interrupted him sternly.

"I don't want to hear one word outta you, old fella. I *told you* that cow was gonna *die*. And if you hadn't got here when you did, neither one of us woulda made any money off of her."

# Moment 4

### Dr. Tweeten Saves the Day

It is quite an adjustment to come from veterinary school to Lamesa, Texas. Dr. Kaccy Tweeten grew up in North Dakota, graduated from Iowa State University, and wound up in Lamesa. Small-town veterinarians fill a niche that includes more than just putting animals back together.

This particular Friday night in West Texas was like all other Fridays in the fall: football night. We go to watch six-man football in the middle of a cotton field, eat hamburgers, and stand around and talk. That's what we do in West Texas.

Steven, the father of one of the cheeleaders, and I were in charge of cooking hamburgers for the home team. The nights were getting chilly, bringing welcome relief from flies and mosquitoes.

I like to take pictures of the football game, so after cooking, I headed for the sidelines. Steven likes to visit. He finished cooking and stood next to the grill, talking about show pigs and farming with anyone who wandered by.

Shortly thereafter, Dr. Tweeten called to inform me that a sick horse was on its way to the clinic. I had a couple of things to do at home, so I left the game to take care of them before the horse arrived and I spent the rest of the evening doing colic surgery.

I had been home only a minute when Kerri called to say that Steven needed some help. I couldn't imagine what it might be. The game was over by now and the burgers long gone.

"A bug flew into his ear, and we can't get it out. Will you meet him at the clinic and see if you can get it out?" Kerri asked.

A bug? It was forty-nine degrees outside. How could a bug fly into someone's ear at that temperature?

"What kind of bug?" I asked, feeling a chuckle coming on.

"A moth. You know, one of those Miller moth things," Kerri replied, as a car door slammed in the background.

"I am at home, but Dr. Tweeten is up there. I will be there in a bit. She can get it out," I replied as the chuckle evolved into an audible giggle.

As I finished my jobs around the house, I found myself laughing aloud. What were the chances of a moth flying into someone's ear? It would have to tuck its body in to fit. I kept picturing the insect zooming in from fifty feet in the air, its wings by its sides like an Olympic diver's arms. Of all the thousands of square feet at that football game, what were the odds that the moth would insert itself into an earhole and not even hit the rim?

I called the clinic on my way in to see what was happening. Dr. Tweeten answered on the first ring and seemed to be stifling a laugh.

"Did you get the bug out of Steven's ear?" I asked, trying to keep from laughing.

"Yep, it was killing him. Seems it wouldn't quit flapping its wings, and the noise and vibration were driving him nuts. It was so deep you couldn't even see it without the otoscope. He was holding his head sideways and pushing on his tragus to keep the thing from banging against his eardrum. I finally got it out. It was bigger than a nickel. I let it go, but he ran and caught it and then stomped it. How in the world could a bug bigger than a nickel dive-bomb and enter an earhole? It was a perfect fit," she said.

By then I was laughing so hard I could barely drive, and Dr. Tweeten was laughing so hard she could barely finish the story.

I am not sure why that is so funny to me, but it is. I am still cracking up as I write this. I guess it is just the fact that a nickel-sized bug could isolate and insert itself into an earhole on a forty-nine-degree night and get in so deep that it required a veterinarian to remove it.

# Moment 5

## Boy and a Hoe

It seems like every plant in West Texas has a thorn, and every animal has a sting. Dry, dusty environments require tough creatures to survive. I have spent my entire life here, so I guess I just assumed that every place was just like here.

Not so. People come here from faraway places, and when they do, they remind me that the whole world is much different from this part of the world.

Dr. Emily is our new intern. She is a feisty, hardworking country girl who moved to West Texas from the Central Valley of California. This little gal works like a sled dog and seemed to be afraid of nothing in the world, but she had never seen a rattlesnake or witnessed the effects of a snakebite on the head of a horse. About a week into her internship, she did. The horse came in looking like they all do: head so swollen it could barely breathe, eyes gooing, and skin splitting. It looked miserable.

She spent a long time looking at this poor critter and commenting how awful it must be to get bitten by one of those slithering varmints. I could see her brain calculating what one of those bites would do to a hundred-pound intern if it did that much damage to a twelve-hundred-pound horse. She nursed that horse through the incident and made many comments about how sorry she felt for it. I could tell she was gaining a healthy respect for, as well as a major fear of, the western diamondback.

A few weeks passed, but the memory of that horse and the dreaded snake did not dim much for Dr. Emily. Her questions focused on the normal habitat of said rattlesnake, and her conversations with clients and other people at the clinic often went to identification and daytime hiding places. One client mentioned that many of the snakes had ceased rattling when startled. His theory was that all the ones that rattled got their heads cut off with a hoe by some cowboy or farmer, and so they had evolved away from the rattle.

This concept worried her even more. How was one to be alerted to one of these toxic beasts if it just set motionless and camouflaged? This seemed to raise her awareness of the environment even more.

One warm July morning, as I walked from one barn to another at the clinic, I heard a faint noise in the distance. The noise was obviously a person, and obviously, that person was in distress. I wasn't sure if the commotion was getting closer to me or if it was just getting louder.

Before I could analyze the exact source completely, I saw the problem. It was Dr. Emily. She was screaming something over and over: "I need a boy and a hoe! I need a boy and a hoe!"

I arrived at the stall she was pointing toward while she danced about and informed me that a giant rattler was in the stall with a horse. Her eyebrows had migrated up to her hairline, and her lips were bent with terror as she continued to call for a hoe before her patient acquired a swollen head.

I saw one of the guys look into the stall at the snake and knew there was no giant rattler when he kind of smiled and started into the stall without the much-needed hoe. Dr. Emily's eyes got even wider as he ambled in and started herding the bull snake back into the pasture.

"What are you doing?" she screeched. "That thing could make your head swell up and cause all the skin to break and your nose holes to collapse! You just gonna run it off? It will come back!"

The fellow just kinda giggled and assured Emily that it was just a rowdy bull snake, and they don't hurt anything, so we don't kill 'em.

"What do you mean they don't hurt anything? I about prolapsed trying to get away from it! That thing was six feet long and hissing, and you're just gonna let it go? It could have given that horse, and *me*, heart failure. *I hate snakes!*"

*twenty*

## Other Vets

# Moment 1

*Dr. Bill*

Dr. Bill is a good friend of mine. He is seventy years old and still practices at a pace that most thirty-year-olds would envy. I talk to him from time to time just to get a reality boost on what I need to do to be like him when I grow up. He is a credit to our profession and an inspiration to me.

A few days ago, we were talking about a horse he was sending to us for surgery, and I mentioned something about prices. I asked him how he went about knowing when it was time to raise prices and how he kept people from having a fit when he did. He proceeded to tell me the story of the cowboy and the dead cows.

A few years back, a couple of old cowboys came into the clinic wanting Dr. Bill to come out to the ranch and post a couple of dead cows. Seems the cows had been dead for an entire day, and the temperature had been over a hundred degrees. The cowboys believed that the cattle had gotten into some oil from local oil-field work, and they wanted Bill to come out, take some samples to send off, and confirm their suspicions. Bill was agreeable. He assured them that he would come out and post the cows within the hour.

As they were heading out the door, one cowboy asked how much it cost to cut up a dead cow. Bill replied that it was $300.

"What? You mean to tell me you gonna charge us almost as much as that cow is worth just to cut her up after she dead? Doc, you're getting to be like them city doctors. That is way too much money to cut up som'in' dead. Why don't you just give me those little sample baggies, and me and Buddy, here, will get them ourselves. What do we got to get?

I'm telling you what, you veterinaries are just gettin' outta control. Last time we had you out to cut up a dead cow, it was just a hundred bucks (even though that was 1976). That is reeediculous."

Bill just smiled and replied, "Sure thing. Here are the baggies, and all you have to do is cut open the cow's paunch and get some of the stuff inside of it out, and put it in this baggy. Then cut into the abdomen, get a foot of small bowel, and put it in this bigger baggy. When you get it, bring it back here, and we will send it off."

A couple of hours later, they showed back up. Neither of them looked too happy, and there was a distinct odor of "dead for too long in the sun" coming off them. Their shirts, which had been a light-blue color on the previous visit, were now an off-green with a crunchy texture from dried goo that had spewed from that bloated creature when they stuck their knife in it to retrieve some paunch juice. Their cowboy hats looked as if someone had blown that bumpy stuff that is on the ceiling of your house all over them, except that the bumpy stuff was green and smelled like a carcass. Their eyes were watering still, and one of them was explaining how he had thrown up three times while driving back to the clinic.

"We decided we wanted you to come do it! We musta done som'in' wrong. That thing blew up like a bomb when we stuck a knife in it. It kept spewing for ten minutes, and every time we would run around to the other side, the wind would change direction, and we would get covered some more. I guess three hundred dollars ain't so bad, considering how nasty a person got to get!"

"How much? No, you misunderstood me. I said three fifty!" dribbled out of Dr. Bill's mouth past a smirky smile and one raised eyebrow.

"That is how you raise prices, Bo. Been doing it like that for forty-five years. No one complains but one time, and then they are glad to pay you!"

# Moment 2

*Dr. Box*

Dr. Ronald Box is a brilliant veterinarian from Pecos, Texas. Ranchers and other veterinarians consider him the go-to doctor for difficult cases in West Texas and New Mexico.

Dr. Box also is a great storyteller. He recently told me of an incident that typifies certain days in the life of a rural veterinarian.

He had pulled up to the locked gate leading into a large, West Texas ranch. The owner was to meet him there, and they were to go down to the pens together to palpate the cows and work the calves.

The owner, a highly successful rancher who had accumulated a fortune and had a passion for cattle ranching, called on Dr. Box to keep the animals healthy at all of his properties.

The owner soon arrived and, after exchanging a few greetings through the rolled-down window of his pickup truck, told Dr. Box to go ahead and open the gate so they could move down to the pens.

Dr. Box, who had not visited this newly purchased ranch before, noticed that someone had shot a hole through the middle of the lock, but it was still holding. He asked for a key, but the owner shouted back that he didn't even know the gate had a lock.

After the doctor spent several minutes trying to jimmy the lock open, the ranch owner grew tired of waiting and stepped out to help. They each pulled a few tools from their trucks and managed to work the lock mechanism to the point that it finally slid open. But it wouldn't swing open quite far enough for them to get the end of the chain loose. That prompted another trip to the toolboxes.

Here stood one man with an excellent college education, and another who'd earned millions in business, but the two of them had now spent more than thirty minutes simply trying to get into the ranch so they could start working. Every attempt was fruitless.

It was beginning to look as though they would have to chop down the gatepost.

They were so absorbed in the task that they hadn't noticed a cowboy ride up on his horse. He had come from the working pens inside to find out why the two were taking so long at the gate. They finally took notice of the cowboy when he spoke.

"The gate opens on the other side," he said, then quietly turned around and rode back to the pens.

Neither Dr. Box nor the rancher had taken the time to observe that they were working on the side of the gate with the hinges. They'd just seen the chain with the lock on it and busied themselves trying to open it.

"A bit humbling" was how Dr. Box described the experience to me.

It's no wonder cowboys and ranch hands think that veterinarians and rich landowners can be a bit goofy at times.

# Moment 3

*Dr. Beaver*

Hands are often a reflection of one's life. They tell a story of how the day is spent and can be decorated with cracks, calluses, and bit-off nails.

I was sitting in the second hour of a board of directors meeting for the Texas Veterinary Medical Association, paying more attention to my hands than to the topic of the moment. Winter always seems to make them uglier than usual. The knuckles get deep, there are bleeding cracks, and the skin seems to get so dry it's probably a fire hazard.

I was looking at the skin on the top of my left hand, and wondering if it was about to dry up and fall off, when the veterinarian sitting to my left pulled out some lotion. She must have seen my hands and been reminded of what truly ugly hands look like.

"Would you mind if I had a little of that?" I asked with the tone of a twelve-year-old asking for some lemonade.

"You don't want any of this; it smells too feminine," she replied with an air of confidence that made me feel as if she was an expert dermatologist. "I've got a different kind in my purse that would work better on those hands."

After digging around for a bit, she pulled out a tube that had "Shea" written on it in bold letters. I was encouraged. I proceeded to squeeze a generous portion into one hand and began to rub it in.

This stuff was amazing, but it never seemed to absorb; it just kinda spread out. After twenty minutes of vigorous rubbing that very well could have been misconstrued as a nervous disorder, my hands were still so slick I could barely pick up my pen.

I tried to wipe some onto the tablecloth, but it didn't want to transfer. In fact, I think I made it angry enough to multiply. The only noticeable change was the blinding sheen that began to form. I could almost see my own reflection.

My next thought was to blow them dry. Like a baseball player in October, I began the procedure, but it was fruitless. I finally gave up.

I wasn't sure what this stuff was, but judging by its staying power, I was pretty sure it would last the rest of the winter.

As the meeting crept into the third hour, I decided to sneak back to the coffee urn for a warm-up, when I heard someone whisper my name.

To my surprise, the president of the American Veterinary Medical Association was just a few feet away. I couldn't believe she knew my name. In fact, I was a bit flabbergasted that someone with her credentials and standing would know a small-town veterinarian from West Texas.

She smiled and extended her hand while I instinctively reached out to greet her. The tighter she gripped my hand, the harder it was to hold on to. It just sort of slid away.

She glanced down to see what she had just grabbed, revealing a polished hand covered in what could have been Crisco. Less than five seconds later, with my cheeks piping hot, I retreated to the coffee table.

I took a little extra time fixing my drink, wondering exactly what she must be thinking. I had some ideas, but I didn't like any of them.

I decided it might be better to just walk out the back door rather than face her again. As I headed to the washroom, I looked over in time to see her rubbing her hand on her tablecloth.

Neither soap nor water was any match for this stuff. Water beaded off my hands as it would a freshly waxed car. I spent the rest of the day trying to avoid anyone I knew and dodging situations where I might be introduced to someone so I could contain the slickest substance known to man.

I was thinking that it would make good bearing grease. Or maybe Olympic bobsled teams could trim a few seconds off their time if they put it on their runners.

At least that AVMA president would never forget me. In fact, she might still have a very shiny, slippery right hand.

# Moment 4

*Blodgett*

The Friday-evening clock read six as Dr. Glenn Blodgett settled into his butt-hungry easy chair to absorb the mindless callings of a football game on ESPN. Things start early at the ranch, and four thirty in the morning is a long time ago to start the day. How wonderful an evening of rest sounded after the stress of running a veterinary clinic for another week.

The evening clock read six thirty when the phone sounded. Seemed a horse was colicking, and the intern was concerned by how fast it had come on and how severe the symptoms were. This was a valuable critter, and ol' Doc figured he should go back to the clinic and put his eyes on it. Shouldn't take but a few minutes, and then the easy chair would welcome him back for the second half of the game.

Great. The colic appeared to be more than medical, and surgery might be needed. Lamesa was a two-hour drive, but it was looking like this horse was gonna need to make the trip. Let's see, if it was 7:00 p.m. then, it would be about nine by the time they got there. About an hour and a half for surgery, another two hours home, he should be tucked comfortably in bed by a little past midnight.

The horse made the trip well and seemed to be almost normal. What then? Dr. Blodgett thought that maybe he should hang out in Lamesa awhile to see if anything changed. Let's see, what did tomorrow hold? Oh yeah, there was an important veterinarian coming to the ranch to interview for a job. She wouldn't be there until nine or ten. If he stayed for an hour or so more and watched, he would still get enough sleep to be reasonably entertaining and hospitable.

Why do things have to be so complicated? An hour of good and then another round of pain. Not the kind of pain that makes you need to head straight to surgery; just enough to keep you from going home.

The clock on the wall of the surgery room read 4:30 a.m. on Saturday when the incision was made to finally start the surgery. The next clock assessment occurred at 7:00 a.m. as the truck pulled out, headed back to Guthrie. Dr. Blodgett would get back in time to take a quick shower and welcome the applying doctor.

His energy level was surprisingly high all day. When the clock struck 3:00 p.m. on Saturday, the good Dr. Blodgett and his applicant were heading for a gathering in a town an hour away. If everything went as planned, he would be in bed by 9:00 p.m., with a mere forty-two or so hours of sleep deprivation.

Of course, the gathering lasted a bit longer than it was supposed to. The normally happy-go-lucky Dr. Blodgett had entered the "hazy zone," which includes moments of raucous laughter followed by moments of blurred understanding and silliness.

The clock on the dashboard read 10:00 p.m. as they left for the one-hour journey home. No more conversation was available to be squeezed from the delicate neurons in the cerebrum of Dr. Blodgett. A word now and then to pierce the silence was all that he could muster.

Finally, the sound of the passenger door closing as the visiting doctor headed for the bunkhouse. All that was left to do was conquer two gates and a garage door, and the good Dr. Blodgett would dissolve into bed.

The first gate required manual opening and closing. Easy enough: put the truck in park, open the gate, drive through, park again, close it, on to the next one. The second gate was even better: just drive up, and the motion detector would sense the approaching vehicle and open itself. The clock read 11:15 p.m. Saturday as Dr. Blodgett approached the last gate on a now-forty-three-hour journey to the bed that called his name.

As luck would have it, the dang thing wouldn't open with just the normal motion detection. He put the truck in park, opened the door... No wait, the gate was opening.

The clock read 11:45 when Dr. Blodgett saw it next. The extent of his awakeness had ended at 11:15 exactly. He fell soundly asleep behind the wheel of the red Ford pickup, which was still running, as the gate opened and closed...He had hit the end.

A mere one hundred yards from his house, the forty-four-hour journey ended. He had spent every ounce of gas in the awake tank, and could no longer hold those eyes open. Thirty minutes of sleep gave him just enough juice to get to the gate, open it again, and dive into that bed.

What a life we veterinarians have. Absolutely amazing.

# Moment 5

### *Salute to Clifford*

It has been almost twenty years since it all began. And I have to thank a skinny surgeon from just north of the Mexico border for showing me the way. It is an amazing story when I look back on it. I never even dreamed it would turn out this way.

Oh, that is not true. I dreamed of it. From as far back as I can remember, I wanted to be a horse surgeon. But it is one of those things that is a bit like that water-looking stuff on the road ahead of you on a hot day—it is always ahead of you, and you never catch it. But Cliff Honnas held that water-looking stuff still long enough that I could actually grab it and thrive.

When I was a fourth-year student at Texas A&M, I was accepted to do an internship at a veterinary school, but I did not take it because it paid $14,000 a year. I had a baby girl and could not figure any way that I could leave Texas and take care of a child on that salary. But I told myself that I would not lose that dream, no matter what. Even if it took thirty years, I was going to be a surgeon who made horses happy. Cliff Honnas...thank God for Cliff Honnas.

Here is what you have to understand. They do not teach you to be a horse surgeon in veterinary school. If you want to do that, you have to go on and do an internship and a residency in that discipline. No one leaves the curriculum at a veterinary school after four years capable of or qualified to do advanced equine surgery. So how is a person to accomplish such a task? Good question.

Human medicine has an answer for this question. It is called privileges. The hospital will grant certain surgical rights to a medical doctor based on training and skill. In veterinary medicine, those don't exist. They don't exist because the veterinarian owns the hospital and is granted rights to do whatever needs to be done at his or her place.

Let me tell you, it is terribly hard to get one of these board-certified horse surgeons to teach a common veterinarian like me how to do these tough surgeries. And I don't blame them. These people went through four years of working day and night at poverty-level pay in order to learn their craft, and they really take offense to some country vet trying to do what they sacrificed so much to accomplish.

But good ol' Cliff always answered the phone. He always took a little time to tell me how to do a surgery when there was no book to explain it or no experience of my own to draw on. That action by Dr. Clifford Honnas has saved a huge number of horses.

Dr. Honnas was a professor at the veterinary school at Texas A&M. He came about the time I left, so I never really met him. I was facing a tough surgery in 1994 and had no clue who I could call to figure out how to get it done. The people who owned this particular horse didn't have much money, and the vet school was seven hours from Lamesa. I happened to have a student from Texas A&M doing an externship at the clinic, and he told me I should call Cliff Honnas. Well, I did, and we were friends from that day forward.

Cliff came to Lamesa a few times to show me how to do difficult procedures. I would pay his way over and give him the surgical fee, and he always seemed perfectly happy with that.

He really didn't come over that many times, but he was always available to talk me through a new procedure. And as time passed, there were fewer and fewer procedures that I hadn't done or didn't knew how to do. But we remained friends.

I never would have been even close to being able to do the things I can presently do without his guidance through those years of uncertainty and doubt. And I really don't think he will ever have any idea how many horses have lived or returned to happiness because of the things he taught me.

Pedro finds his way into the Cliff Honnas story because he was also a figure who changed my history. He was a Spanish fella from a town about an hour away who started using me as a veterinarian long before I knew what I was doing.

This fella had confidence in me as a horse doctor and brought race-horses for me to work on at least once a week. We had worked together to keep his horses running fast for a couple of years when one of them obtained a chip in its left knee. At the time, I did not do arthroscopic surgery.

One of my classmates, John Vandermeer, had a plethora of arthro-scopes. His father was the team doctor for the Dallas Cowboys, and John sent me a few arthroscopes because he knew I had a passion for learning to fix horses. All he sent were the scopes. I had no light source, no fluid pump, no camera or screen, no surgery table, no money to get those things, and worst of all...I didn't know how to do it.

Pedro saw the radiograph and told me he would leave the horse for me to take the chip out. I told him I didn't have all the stuff to do it and didn't have the money it would take to buy all that expensive stuff.

Pedro couldn't believe it. I guess he just thought every vet knew how to do that stuff. He asked how much it would cost to get the rest of the stuff I would need to take out the chip. I told him the bare minimum for used equipment would be a couple thousand dollars. He never even blinked. He told me he was gonna leave the horse and pay me $2,000 for the surgery and that I could use it to buy what I needed.

Great! What was I going to do now? Just having an airplane doesn't make one a pilot. I had a horse, all the equipment I needed, the desire, and no knowledge. In came Honnas. By then, we had become friends, and my only hope was some instruction and some luck.

Cliff answered the phone call on the first ring. I told him my situa-tion, and he immediately went into a detailed description of what I was about to face and how to get it done, much like he would have with a resident at the vet school. He described it with a calm and easy attitude, tossing in an occasional joke along the way to lower my blood pressure.

I listened closely and studied the anatomy deeply over a few days. All of the equipment arrived, and I—along with some of the best supporting cast on Earth—went to work. It just so happened to be the easiest chip there is to get out of a joint, and we got that rascal out like we had been doing arthroscopy for years.

Serendipity played a role in that moment. It just so happened to be the absolute easiest chip to clean up that a horse can get. It just so happened that Honnas was kind enough to share with me a procedure that wasn't described in any book that was available at the time. I was lucky enough to find a "human" doctor who had just the equipment lying around that I needed for exactly $2,000. And it just so happened that Pedro had total confidence in a small-town doctor to fix his horse.

That horse went on to win about $50,000. Pedro trained about 150 horses and was well connected with dozens of trainers who eventually would use our service for arthroscopic surgery.

What a blessing. That one surgery resulted in the biggest change in my career that would ever happen. Over the next twenty years, I would go on to do thousands of arthroscopic surgeries. I never had a lesson from anyone but Honnas, and to this day have never even seen anyone do an arthroscopy but him.

I am not totally sure how many people Dr. Honnas has taught to do those surgeries, but I am fairly sure that none of them has done as many as I have. Because he took the time to answer that phone call, a huge number of horses have gone on to run fast and be happy.

So, here is to Clifford Honnas. No book by me would be complete without a chapter thanking him for being my friend.

# Moment 6

*Britt*

I try never to judge people by the clothes they wear or the cars they drive, but after eleven years of getting hot checks and no-pay clients, you start paying attention to the subtle clues that might mean you are about to lose some money.

It was 11:58 a.m. when this fellow drove up in an orange Pinto.

We have been blessed over the years with many veterinary students, and we consider it a privilege to be a part of their training. This particular summer found us with Britt Conklin. Dr.-to-Be Conklin was a go-getter and always accused me of being the biggest pessimist in the world.

It had been about three straight weeks of working through lunch, and I was really looking forward to eating and resting just a bit before the busy afternoon got started. But instead, in walked the occupant of the orange Pinto. He was wearing a T-shirt that was so old it had a "runner" in it. At his side was a German shepherd that was so skinny you could read a newspaper through him. The only thing on this dog that wasn't totally devoid of normal size was his abdomen. This critter's belly was twice as big around as anything else and just kinda jiggled as the dog ambled to the front door of the clinic.

As usual, Britt dove in. He filled out a record and took the motley pair into the exam room to work his healing magic. I went to my office and began pouting over another missed lunch.

In a few minutes, he was at the door of the office, listing his findings: heart murmur, congested lungs, ascites, and pallor were just a few of the ailments that came rolling off his highly educated tongue.

"What do you think is wrong, Dr. Brock?" was his final sentence as his eyebrows drifted up his forehead.

"What do I think is wrong?" I replied in a sarcastic tone. "That dog has practically got a heartworm crawling out of his nose. Before you do anything to that dog, you make sure the owner of the Pinto understands that the dog is in terrible shape and most likely won't live. Remember, we have to treat those dogs with arsenic to kill the worms, and one that is that sick will have a hard time. If he does decide he wants to treat him, make sure you get a deposit."

"Here you go being a pessimist again," bubbled out of his lips. as his eyebrows made the trip back to the normal position. "You never know what might happen, and you never know how much this guy loves his dog."

He was right. I was feeling a bit guilty about my judgments. But I couldn't help thinking that if this guy loved this dog so much, why did he let it turn into a walking skeleton before he brought it in? And as for the money thing, well, treating heartworms is an expensive proposition. It takes very expensive medicine, eight or so weeks of confinement, and serial blood tests to monitor the progress of the patient. Maybe this guy was really a millionaire who just chose to drive an orange Pinto, but I was doubting it.

A confident "Let me take care of this" met my ears, and off Britt went.

A few minutes later, he returned with a smile, the news of a deposit, and a signed slip of permission to treat the dog for the now-confirmed case of heartworms. I was feeling even more guilty now.

We routinely run an initial blood test to evaluate whether the dog can tolerate the treatment. This dog was in terrible shape. We decided to treat the other concurrent problems with the liver and kidneys before we subjected the dog to the worm-killing dose of arsenic.

Much to my surprise, the next day found a totally different dog. He could stand up on his own, was actually wagging his tail, and was eating and drinking like nobody's business. I was beginning to feel some "crow eating" coming on as Britt told me how well the dog had responded to the initial treatment.

All I had to say was, "What kind of odds did you give this guy?"

"Well, yesterday I told him there was a less than 30 percent chance that the dog would live. But when he called this morning, I upped it to 70 percent. He was so excited that he said he would be down in a little while to see."

Just as he had told me, the fellow showed up, and they just went on and on about how well things were going. The Pinto driver shook Britt's hand for a good long time, and he departed the clinic with the largest smile I had seen in a while. I could smell the crow cooking as Britt stuck his chest out and returned to the side of his patient.

So far, we had run seventy-five dollars' worth of blood tests, given fifty dollars' worth of medications, run twenty dollars' worth of heart-worm tests, put in a catheter, and run forty-five dollars' worth of fluids. Remember, we hadn't even started treating the heartworms yet. I still had my doubts, but Britt spent the entire day walking with a hop in his step.

The next morning, we walked to the kennel together to check out the progress of that dog. The situation was a little bit different than it had been the day before. That dog was so dead that it was unbelievable. His legs were stiff and poking through the side of the kennel.

"What am I going to do? This guy thinks his dog is doing great!" shrieked Britt. "How could that dog have died? He was doing great just twelve hours ago. Now he is lying there as if he died two weeks ago! Oh my gosh! This is terrible!"

Britt did not have a hop in his step as he went to the phone. Doom and gloom were written all over his face as he solemnly told Mr. Pinto the bad news.

For the rest of the summer, Britt was a man of percentages. He couldn't give a vaccination without saying that there was a 30 percent chance the dog may die. By the end of the summer, I started calling him the eternal pessimist. He informed me that it was a lot easier to tell someone who was expecting his or her dog to die that it had lived than it was to explain how one that was supposed to live had died.

"No kidding," was my reply as I put the first bite of crow into his mouth.

A few days later, when the tenderness of the situation had dulled, I told him that all was not lost: at least he'd gotten a deposit.

"Oh, I was going to tell you about that," Britt said. "Mr. Pinto only had ten dollars on him that day."

# Moment 7

*Dr. Mark*

Dr. Mark Justice explained the events of the previous night with a mixture of regret and relief. I had met the horse in question before, and nothing he could have said would have surprised me. The critter was huge and stupid. When I say huge, I am not joking. This thing was over sixteen hands tall and must have weighed fourteen hundred pounds. That wasn't the bad part. The horse was spoiled by its owner and would kick, bite, paw, and demolish anyone who made it do anything it wasn't in the mood to do.

Mark had been called out the night before to repair a giant laceration on the horse. The following events led up to his referring the horse to us in Lamesa. And he was calling to apologize.

At sunset, the owner called Mark. She was in hysterics. Her horse had run into something in the pasture and sustained an eighteen-inch slash on the front of its rear left leg. The cut was close to a joint and had severed a large blood vessel. Blood was squirting, and muscle tissue was hanging out. The owner was in tears when she met Mark at the truck. She was panicked as she described the situation. Little did he know what he was getting into.

Since it was after hours, Mark asked his new bride to go along and see what a typical farm call was like. She followed him over fences and through barns until they came to the critter in question. The owner was right: the cut was deep and in a dangerous place. But she had failed to tell Mark about the look in the horse's eyes. Having worked on thousands of horses, Mark knew when one might be a bit snakey. This horse was snakey, and Mark could tell it from across the pasture.

After about fifteen minutes of chasing and sweet-talking, he finally got a halter on the beast. When he stuck the needle into the vein to give the sedative, the horse reared up, pawed, and tried to bite him. He decided that it might be prudent to up the dose a bit. Even with an elephant dose of sedative, the horse was still kicking at him when he tried to clean the wound. So Mark gave more.

Let me paint the picture here: Mark was standing in the middle of a pasture with only the lights of a pickup to see what he was doing. A frantic owner and Mark's new bride looked on; each worried about one of the parties involved. The horse was so tranquilized it could barely stand, but it still kicked with fly-swatting accuracy. Mark had given an elephant dose—plus one—and now was trying a local block with lidocaine around the area so he could suture the laceration.

He gently slid the needle holding the numbing agent into an area of the skin that needed to be sutured. To his surprise, the horse just stood there. Maybe the sedative had finally worked! When he started instilling the medicine, the horse suddenly kicked. The kick hit his hand and sent the syringe flying twenty yards across the pasture, where it stuck in a pecan tree. So he gave some more sedative.

Funny thing about that sedative—it makes a male horse extend his "boy part." After the third dose of sedative, the critter finally let him instill the local anesthesia, but now the boy part was hanging down, right in the way of the suturing job. It was hitting Mark all over his head as he tried to sew.

Do you know how hard it is to squat down and sew up a horse but remain in a position that allows for a quick exit if the situation calls for it? Do you know how hard that is with the added complication of a boy part slapping you in the face? The good doctor finally had enough and reached over to move the annoying part. This, of course, caused another vicious kick that sent the needle flying into the darkness of the pasture. The new bride was getting concerned, the owner was apologizing, and Mark was giving another dose of sedative.

With both hands bruised, a missing pair of needle holders, a syringe stuck in a pecan tree, a worried wife, and a nagging owner, Mark decided it was time to send this horse to Lamesa, where there was a set of stocks and a way to anesthetize the monster fully.

The next day, his voice was filled with regret and relief. All I could do was laugh as I listened to him apologize for sending me such a mess.

# Moment 8

*Five Pounds*

After twenty-five years of giving public talks, there ain't too many situations I let myself get into that are going to be risky. There are just some crowds that I don't want to talk to and some places I just don't fit in. About six months after graduating from vet school, I hadn't figured this out yet.

I stood at a podium in front of about four hundred cattle raisers and proceeded to give a talk on injection-site lesions. Crap, I didn't know anything about them, but I had been asked to do it, and so I did. I had researched and studied enough that I thought I was qualified. But man oh man, was I wrong. The crowd obviously sensed this. After I talked, they began to ask me questions that were so difficult that Alex Trebek would have had no idea.

One man in particular was just wearing me out. I was about twenty-six, and he was about sixty. He could see that I had little experience, and he was really enjoying watching me sweat and stutter every time he asked a new question. Heck, I didn't know the answer to even one of his questions, and half of them had nothing to do with what I was talking about at all.

This went on and on. I couldn't believe that someone on the panel of "experts" couldn't see my suffering and end my section of the talk. They all just sat there with dumb looks on their faces and watched me be eaten alive. By the time the sixty-year-old got through with me, I was a babbling mess. I finally went back to my station on the elongated table on the stage at the front of the room and vowed never to give a public talk again. There were four more panelists to go after me. This meant that I had to set in front of this crowd and be glared at by Mr. Sixty-Year-Old for at least another hour.

The next fella who spoke gave an incredibly boring talk about some random cattle-feeding principle. I don't think I heard a word he said because my brain was still spinning from the thirty-minute volley of unanswerable questions. He finished and politely asked if there were any questions.

This was just what Sixty was waiting for. That rascal let loose on the boring speaker and asked him another round of stupid and meaningless questions that he couldn't answer either. Jeez, what a turdhead. I felt a little bit better for myself because at least I wasn't the only idiot on the panel, but I couldn't help feeling sorry for my fellow panelist because the latest questions were even more insulting and difficult.

This same scenario played out after the next two speakers took the podium. Ol' Sixty tore them up too. I was amazed at how rude this fella was, and my emotions had moved from insecurity to anger. He was just loving making a fool out of every person on that panel and by now, he had become annoying to most of the people in the audience too.

Dave was the last speaker. He was a PhD in some discipline and was doing research on IBR in feedlot cattle. Dave was no neophyte to public speaking. He was quick-witted and a marvelous speaker. He was getting close to sixty years of age himself, and I sensed no fear in his stride as he strolled toward the podium to present the conclusions of his recent research.

I felt a bit sorry for Dave even before any words came forth from his mouth. I knew Mr. Sixty was gonna let loose on anything that had to do with the already controversial subject of IBR in cattle. I didn't figure Dave would get a quarter of the way into his talk before he was interrupted with a know-it-all question from Sixty.

Dave went to work. He began by introducing some facts about IBR and how the research trial had been designed. He has a marvelous way of using his voice to keep listeners' attention and a pleasant sense of humor that kept people interested. I was watching the expression on Mr. Sixty's face. This great speaking style seemed to tick him off even more. I could tell that he was about to boil over every time Dave gave another fact or finding. After watching Sixty for four speakers now, I had determined that he just couldn't stand it if *he* wasn't the center of attention, and Dave was stealing the show.

Dave said that during the trial, the researchers had noticed three things early on about cattle that were infected with a field strain of IBR. He said that all ran a temperature of over 104 degrees, all went off feed for the first four days, and all lost five pounds.

I was looking at the sixty-year-old heckler when that statement came out of Dave's mouth. Mr. Heckler's face twisted up as if he had just taken a bite of a lemon, and he leaped to his feet to holler out his latest statement/question.

"Dr. Dave, I cannot believe that a man with your scientific background would even make a statement like that. Don't you know that a calf can lose five pounds just due to the stress of running through a squeeze chute?"

I looked over at Dave. I was expecting to see an expression similar to the one that had been on my face and those of Mr. Sixty's other three victims. But to my surprise, he was calm as a cucumber and began a verbal reply almost as quickly as the last words came from Sixty's mouth.

"You are correct, sir!" Dave replied with a tone of complete confidence. "These were five-hundred-pound cattle that we were working with, and we ran one of them through the chute a hundred times, and he *disappeared!*"

This resulted in complete and total laughter from the audience. I mean hard laughter. Not the kind that lasts for a couple of seconds and dissipates. No, the kind that kinda wanes for a second, and then gets loud again in undulating waves that continue for minutes. I was leading the laughter charge from the podium, and the other panelists were chiming in at high volumes mixed with occasional knee slaps.

The expression on Mr. Sixty's face was the absolute best part of the entire story. Words cannot describe the emotion that was displayed on that fella's mug as the entire crowd rejoiced at his expense. His skin tone went from a morbid whitish-gray to radish-red, highlighted with purple on his cheeks.

His eyebrows went from the very top of his forehead while he was spouting off the know-it-all question to just above his eye sockets as the crowd laughed and pointed at him. His ears went back like those of a mad mare not in heat next to a stud with ideas she wasn't fond of.

His posture deteriorated to a hunker, and he folded his arms on the table in front of him. He seemed to shrink in size from this incredibly large man to the stature of a fifth-grade boy who had just been sent to the principal's office. I could tell by his body language that we weren't gonna hear from Mr. Sixty again that day.

Dave finished his talk on IBR. It went superbly. I still remember some of his findings and use them in practice today. There was not another peep from the crowd, and the panel talk ended with a round-table discussion that was productive and informative. As for ol' Sixty... there was not even a peep.

I went up to Dave after the thing had ended and told him that he was my hero. There is nothing I like better than quick wits and clever. I will never forget that day and still consider Dave to be one of the coolest dudes I have ever met. I am not sure what happened to Sixty. I never saw or heard from him again. But I can guarantee you this: he learned his lesson that day about messing with Dave, the IBR man.

*twenty one*

# Boo-Boos

# Moment 1

### Turning Fifty

I turned fifty just recently. Eeesh. I got out of the shower that day and just stood in front of the mirror, trying to see what twenty-four years of being a veterinarian had done to this body. (I know you are probably grossing out thinking about me out of the shower and in front of a mirror. So am I.) But I evaluated the effects of working on animals that weigh as much as a Volkswagen.

My feet...well, the left one was stepped on by a horse and has never really been the same since. The skin on the top of that foot peeled off and left this scar-looking thing that itches like crazy in the winter. Another horse stepped on my right foot, and now the big toe looks like a comma on steroids. The metatarsus that leads to it has a callus on the bone where the same horse broke it, but I just never got it fixed because I was too busy to go to the doctor.

The left knee bends both ways because I was trying to load a stupid racehorse into a trailer, and it backed over it. I feel sure that there were many things that professional football players have surgery on that needed to be fixed, but once again, I was just too busy. That left knee stayed swollen all the time; it is about twice the size of my right knee.

The horse kick to the belly resulted in surgery to put about ten inches of mesh over the torn muscles and hernia that resulted. But once again, I was so busy that I went back to work and did a colic surgery two days after the good doctor, Beth, put me back together. This, of course, resulted in a much more fibrous scar than it should have been, but it held together, so I just kept on working.

The gallbladder went to crap a few years back. Can't blame that on an animal, but it probably resulted from eating junk food every day for lunch and breakfast for twenty-four years because I was too busy to stop and eat right. That left a series of scars that look like a smiley face with just one eye.

That neuro exam on a two-year-old horse left my right thumb broken, and it will bend only toward the palm. For about a year, I had to use my left hand to pull it away from the other fingers, or it would stay there all the time. I went to the doctor for that one, and he wanted to do surgery, but I told him just to put a cast on it because I didn't have time to go to the hospital for a surgery.

I have to thank a series of people who have worked with me over the years for sewing me up multiple times. I would be kicked or smashed in the squeeze chute, and they would just throw me down on the couch in my office and suture me up. Both of my hands and arms are covered with scars from these episodes because I never went to the doctor...yes, because I didn't have time.

The old back was broken in seven places...not by a horse, but in a car wreck I sustained while driving to work. When the ambulance arrived, I told the EMTs that I would go to the hospital as soon as I got done with the surgery I was driving to the clinic to do. Thank goodness, they wouldn't let me.

The top of my head has a scar that is about eight inches long from the same episode. The scar is huge and folded over itself because I got someone at work to take all the staples out instead of going to the doctor because I just didn't have time to miss work.

My left butt cheek has a permanent dimple in it where a cow smushed me against a palpation gate and tore some muscle that makes up my now-barely existent fanny. The same bun has a scar where another cow horned me as I was trying to run away.

My left shoulder has no muscle left on the back of it since I was bitten by a filly after her owner assured me that she never bit anyone. I have skin precancers and rosacea all over my face from standing outside day after day watching horses trot.

## Chapter Twenty One

I have brucellosis from when I stuck myself with a strain-19 vaccine in 1991 on a big ranch in the middle of nowhere and wound up being sick every night about bedtime for twelve years.

But overall, I would say I am pretty lucky. I am fifty and, as of today, still going strong. I just thank God every day that he has let me do what I love to do for so long.

# Moment 2

*Kidney*

Sometimes it is good for the doctor to be the one being doctored. It is a small reminder of what those critters are going through while we are trying to get them well. I had an event like this a few years ago that kept me tuned in to pain and treatments.

I was watching a football game and waiting for church time to come around, when suddenly, it felt like someone sneaked into my room and kicked me in the stomach. The primitive part of my brain registered, *Sharp pain going on in the midgut area, Bo*, while the logic part of my brain theorized, *No one could have snuck in here and kicked me in the stomach without me seeing him.*

I figured it would just go away in a second. But the pain just kept building and building. I was starting to just kinda curl up. Pretty soon, my knees were approaching my chin. What was happening? I remembered those classes we took while Kerri was pregnant. *In through your mouth, out through your nose*, I thought. *Hoo-hoo-heehoo-hoo-hee.* It wasn't helping.

Here it was late December, and I was pouring sweat from every gland in my body. I was thinking about those horses with colic, and how they just drip with sweat when their pain intensifies. Intense pain was an understatement; I was lying in a puddle on the floor when Kerri came in to ask me if I was ready for church.

Church? Are you kidding? I'm not sure I can stand. A mere ten minutes had passed since the phantom had sneaked into the room and kicked me in the stomach, but it seemed as though I had been hunched over for hours.

"What's the matter with you?" she asked with concern in her eyes.

I dribbled something about a steel-toe-boot-wearing phantom who had had his way with me.

We substituted the hospital for church. I had no idea what was happening, but I knew that if I didn't get some relief soon, I was going to dehydrate from sweating.

The woman at the front desk must have seen this hunkered-over gait before: bent over at the waist, hands curled around the midsection, profuse sweating accompanied by a mild moan with each exhale.

"Oh, passing a kidney stone, I see," she said matter-of-factly.

Was that what was happening to me? I'd heard about these, and I knew things were going to get worse.

Once I was home, things were better. They sent me home with pain medicine and a paper cup in which to catch the rascal. I was gonna catch it and have it bronzed. This thing must be as big as a grapefruit, I thought. And when it was born, I was going to preserve it for posterity.

The pain medicine kept me a bit stoned all night, so I didn't really look in the cup at the end of each visit to the bathroom. The folk at the hospital had given me some fluids, so I must have gone five or six times throughout the night.

I was feeling much better when morning broke. That thing must have passed, and I knew it was in that paper cup in the bathroom. I couldn't wait to see the monster. I snatched up the paper cup, and there it was: huge and brown with spikes all over it. No wonder this thing hurt so bad.

"Kerri, come have a look at this beast," I called. "It must be the granddaddy of all kidney stones."

"That's not a kidney stone," she said with a confused look on her face.

After further examination, it seemed that some poor bug had wandered into the cup at some point in the night, and I had blown it to pieces, leaving just one leg attached to its body. The real stone was there, too. At the very bottom of the cup was a little comma.

"A comma?" That little thing caused all this? I would need to rethink my bronzing idea.

I often think about being doubled over in pain as I doctor critters. Now I've got a better idea of what it's like not to know what is going on when you go see the doctor.

# Moment 3

### Broken Arm

"Useless as a one-armed paperhanger."
That's how my grandfather would describe me when I seemed to be all thumbs while trying to do certain jobs.

Not long ago, the metaphor came true after a manic racehorse kicked my right hand and broke my thumb. "Useless" may be the best way to describe a veterinarian who can't use his right thumb. "Frustrated" is what I'd call it.

Though I didn't miss any surgeries or turn anyone away, having only four exposed fingers on my right hand (and I am right-handed) made everything take twice as long. My thumb, wrist, palm, and upper forearm were held tightly in place by a heavy, rigid cast.

One day, I already had been on several emergency calls and was ready for the workday to end. I was driving to this last farm, hoping the job wouldn't take long. The owner of a donkey had told me the baby had its head and one leg out, but the other leg was still inside, and things had gone south.

I pulled up to find a female miniature donkey standing in a muddy pen, just as he described. What he hadn't mentioned was that the baby appeared to be as large as its mother was. In fact, it looked like a donkey with two heads, one at each end, and each about the same size. I realized this was going to take more than a few minutes.

I've known the owner, a senior gentleman, for years and consider him a good friend. But, truth be told, I was thinking that he probably wouldn't be much help as I started trying to deliver this baby one-handed.

He held the lead rope with a regretful, worried look on his face. That was all he could do—hold the rope and offer words of encouragement as I struggled. And struggle I did. This thing was whipping me. I pulled, tugged, grunted, groaned, got pulled through the mud, stepped on, and rolled on as I tried to get that other leg out of the four hundred-pound donkey using mostly my left hand.

After thirty minutes, the leg was in the exact place it was when we started. I needed a break. I went back to the pickup truck to regroup. My left arm was cramping, and my cast was broken. My glasses were caked with afterbirth, and this donkey had dragged me enough to fill my underwear and trousers with dirt and straw.

I hadn't had mud in the creases of my body since I went to the beach as a little kid. I didn't like it then, and I didn't like it now. It was squishing around as I sat in the truck and called my wife to let her know I'd be late.

Finally, during the thirty-minute second round, the leg popped out. I started celebrating as if I'd just won a gold medal. All I had to do now was pull the baby the rest of the way out, and everything would be fine.

Wrong.

It still wouldn't come out. The jenny had lain down, so when I pulled on the baby, she'd just drag us around the pen. I couldn't hold her and pull the baby at the same time, so I asked the owner if any neighbors were around who might give us a hand.

There were. About twenty minutes later, a man—like the owner, a bit past middle age—showed up to assist. We all tried for a while and decided we needed more reinforcements. Soon the owner's grandson (about my age) arrived. That was all we needed. Some pulled, and some held, and the baby finally came the rest of the way out.

The momma donkey did just fine. I was a mess. A good shower got the layer of guck off my frazzled body. I had not been that dirty since childhood.

One of the benefits of being a veterinarian is that you can simply make yourself a new cast when the old one breaks.

Just another exciting day in the life of a small-town practitioner.

*twenty two*

## At the Clinic

# Moment 1

*Boogers*

A mixed-animal veterinary clinic holds a large number of distractions for the casual observer.

Many clients, who are just passing through with a pet or a large animal that needs attention, don't spend enough time with us to become used to all the clinic sights, sounds, and smells—or to the doctor's mannerisms. Any number of small things can distract them while you are trying to describe what's wrong with their animal.

For example, there's nothing worse than giving a long explanation about how to medicate a pet at home, only to discover later that an unsightly particle of debris in your nose probably hypnotized the client half the time you were talking.

That's why we developed a "booger" signal among our staff. It's just a subtle change in facial expression, followed by a mock scratching of the right or left nostril to alert the offender.

The way our clinic is set up, you have to go through the waiting room to get suture material from one of the exam rooms.

This particular day, when I was about halfway through a C-section on a cow, I was in a mad dash from the cattle chute to get a spool of suture. The palpation sleeves I was wearing were covered in blood and guck all the way to my shoulders.

As luck would have it, I encountered a very short woman at the waiting-room entrance. She had a question, and it was very apparent that she was going to ask it *right now*. She pulled me over, blood-covered as I was, and started firing questions about her dog.

I was really in a hurry to get back to the gaped-open cow, and assumed that she could tell that I was in the middle of surgery, but she was interested only in getting her questions answered and paid no attention to the blood dripping down the sleeves and front of my coveralls.

I caught sight of Berenda, our office manager, standing off to one side. For a split second, my attention left the rapid-fire questions and focused on her.

Berenda was making the booger signal.

The woman with the questions was perhaps five feet tall. I stand about six feet. This meant that she had a clear and unobstructed view of my nostrils. She was so short that no amount of head bowing on my part was going to obscure her view. And, with my hands and arms covered to the shoulders with the cow's fluids, I couldn't wipe my nose or even brush it against my shoulder.

Berenda seemed to find my predicament amusing. Out of the corner of my eye, I saw her laughing as I moved from one awkward position to another, trying to find one that would allow me to look at the woman without exposing too much of my nose.

Berenda would shake her head each time I moved my head, as if to alert me that "it" was still visible to the client.

Finally, the woman finished with her questions and left.

Berenda was laughing hysterically now. "You don't have a booger," she said. "My nose was just itching, and you happened to look over as I was scratching it. You mistook that for the signal, and I didn't know how to call it off. Maybe we need another signal to cancel out the accidental one."

That's what she told me, but deep down, I have to wonder if she just wanted to see me go through the eleven basic ballet movements while trying to hide my nose without being able to touch it.

# Moment 2

## Mr. Ford

We prefer to do surgery in the morning—my favorite time of day—before the telephone starts ringing and emergencies begin showing up. It's peaceful, and surgery usually can be done without hurry or distraction.

Our clinic is a place that some of the townsfolk like to hang out, perhaps while a flat is getting fixed or rain has stopped their work for a while.

One older gentleman, Mr. Ford, would stop by regularly to watch surgery, even though we often start as early as 6:00 a.m.

This particular morning was chilly, so Manda stoked up our little gas heater to add some warmth to the surgery room. The thing fits on top of a propane bottle and gets red-hot.

Mr. Ford was there as usual, and he was a talker. He loved to tell stories, some from his World War II days. We'd heard most of them many times. If someone came in with a horse, he might tell the one about the prize racehorse he ran in 1955; I'd heard that one a thousand times. Some people would walk away, but others would listen for perhaps thirty minutes or more. He loved it. It was what he lived for. I never complained. It gave clients something to do while they waited, and it made him happy.

That morning, he was standing in front of the red-hot heater, talking about how smart his dog was. Being familiar with that one, too, most of us had tuned him out for the moment as we fished around in a horse's knee for a bone chip.

I'm not sure who smelled it first, but we all looked up at the same time.

Something was burning.

About that time, Mr. Ford, in a calm and casual voice, said, "I'm on fire."

He had backed into the heater until his britches touched the hot grill and began to burn. Smoke was coming from just above the bend of his knee. He was patting himself on the back pockets, trying to put it out. At eighty-four years of age, bending down that low is perhaps more painful than being on fire.

Everyone in the room went into fire mode. Manda started beating the burning pants with a towel, but that just seemed to stoke the heat and create more smoke. The fire grew worse as others in the room looked about for something else to put it out. I was thinking of throwing Mr. Ford on the ground and rolling him around, but decided that might hurt him. Besides, I was sterile for the surgery. We needed water, but there was none to be found—unless we picked him up and put him in the sink.

Then it hit me.

I pulled the arthroscope out of the cannula and aimed it at Mr. Ford's leg. Manda saw it happening and turned up the pressure on the pump to high. The lavage fluid hit the burning pants, and in seconds, the fire was out. I realized that I never broke sterility.

It was all just a comma to Mr. Ford, who, calm as a cucumber, resumed the story about his dog exactly where he had left off while the rest of us were coming down from our adrenaline rush.

Mr. Ford passed away a few months back. We all miss him and his many interesting tales. But what we'll remember most is that chilly morning when his trousers caught fire.

I can't help but wonder how many surgeons can say they've extinguished a burning pair of pants with an arthroscope and never broken sterility?

# Moment 3

*Persnickety*

The dictionary defines this word as "placing too much emphasis on trivial or minor details." I have been practicing veterinary medicine for twenty years, and through that window of time, my definition of "minor details" has changed.

I have quoted the life cycle of heartworm and the pathogenesis of navicular disease so many times that I am bored to death with it. As far as I am concerned, it is a trivial detail, and I never want to tell the story again. But most people have never heard either of those stories, and it is not a minor detail to them.

But it is not that type of minor detail that drives me nuts; it is that client who comes in with a list. Oh my, I hate lists. When I see a client pull one out, i just want to prolapse. I know that there is about to be a twenty-minute question-and-answer session, and that every answer I give will be researched on the Internet and among the checkers at PetSmart and the bag loaders at the feed store.

For example, one list-bearing banker dude is the epitome of persnickety. I dispensed some antibiotic tablets for his dog to be given twice a day. The next day he called me up.

"Yes, ahhhh, Dr. Brock, ahhhh, I was just calling with a question on the dosing of the antibiotic you sent home with my poodle yesterday. I hate to be a stickler, but according to the dosage schedule on the manufacturer's website, ahhhh, Missy should be getting thirteen-thirty-seconds of a tablet twice a day, and I believe you had us giving a half of a tablet."

True story.

What? Are you kiddin' me? I am talking to a banker about drug calculations, and he has corrected me? This guy got on the Internet, found the website, got the dosage schedule, calculated the dose, and came up with a fraction of a tablet that has the numbers thirteen and thirty-two in it?

I started to try to justify my "overdosage" by using some big, medical diatribe and trumping his Internet with my education. But then, I decided to play along. I just told him to hang on a minute while I recalculated the dose. I then proceeded to tell him that he was correct and that he needed to break each tablet into thirty-two equally sized portions and then give the dog thirteen of those portions twice a day. I apologized for being off a bit in my calculation and said that the slight overdose was not dangerous to the dog in any way. I went on to tell him that it was very important that each of the thirty-two portions be exactly the same size.

There was a long moment of quiet as he absorbed the matter. I wasn't sure what was going through his mind, but I was on the edge of my seat waiting for the result. What prompts a person to hang on to such a detail? Had he not even considered for a minute the absurdity of such a calculation? Did he just want to call and show me how smart he was, or did he actually think that I was an idiot who could not calculate a dose?

Instead of admitting defeat, he replied, "How would one go about breaking up one of those small tablets into thirty-two equal portions?"

"I have no idea. Maybe you should just break it in half and pretend that six thirty-seconds of the thing flaked off when it broke," I replied.

This made him laugh. He laughed and laughed until I was beginning to get uncomfortable.

Finally, after what seemed like a good two minutes of fake-sounding laughter, he replied, "I guess that brings us right back to where we started. Wow, I guess that is why I am a banker and not a doctor, huh?"

*You got that right, you persnickety-sounding rascal*, was what I was thinking as he began another round of strange laughter. I had just spent ten minutes on the phone facing too much emphasis on minor, or trivial, details.

# Moment 4

*GI Joe*

Everyone calls him Pink. I have no idea what his real name is; he has always just been Pink to me. He comes into the clinic with his Chihuahuas, and as long as I have been in Lamesa, we have been friends.

He must be around eighty-five years old now, though it seemed like he was that old twenty years ago when I came to Lamesa. He is just one of those fellas who must have been born looking eighty-five and never got any older. He has an opinion about everything and is not afraid to express it.

When he comes to the clinic, he stays for hours. He will just set in the waiting room with one of his five or six dogs and talk to everyone who comes in. He has stories about the war (not sure if he was actually in one or just heard about it), stories about farming cotton (he never farmed in his life), stories about police work (he has a grandson who was a policeman), and stories about his dogs and all the smart things they can do (they are absolutely not smart).

This particular day found a group of local farmers gathered in the lobby of the clinic looking at a dog that had gotten into paraquat, a defoliant that the farmers around here use. This dog had somehow managed to get into it big-time. It was a great big dog, and they had carried that thing into the lobby and just set it on the floor right in the middle of the room.

Pink was there with his favorite Chihuahua, Monster, tucked under his left arm. He was telling how that stuff was like the Agent Orange they had sprayed in Vietnam. He was going on and on about all the things it did and how it had killed billions of soldiers years later.

I was examining the dog and listening to all the country folk go over the vast amount of trivial knowledge that seemed to be stored up in their brains about defoliants. I really couldn't remember everything I needed to know about paraquat, so I announced that I was going to my office to get Dr. Bailey's notes from vet school.

These people remind me of Cliff Clavin on *Cheers*. They know everything about everything and seem to want to top each other with another level of BS just as soon as there is a momentary pause in conversation. I had heard about all I could stand, and going for the notes looked like a good way to catch my thoughts in peace and not have to listen to them endlessly topping one another with war stories and farming practices.

Pink was leading the BS competition by a large margin when I left for the office. He was making a highly technical comparison of the paraquat and Agent Orange theories and rebuking the farmers for letting the dog get into it. I found the notes and decided just to carry them out to the lobby with me. I knew that whatever I said was gonna be scrutinized, and I figured it would save a trip back to the office to prove my point if I just took the notes with me.

I arrived back at the giant, sickly dog with notes wide open. I began reading them aloud to the group after having given the credentials of Dr. Bailey as the world's greatest animal toxicologist. The very first thing that was stated in the notes was something that made ol' Pink's head swell up: "defoliant similar to Agent Orange" was a part of the first sentence. He looked like a banty rooster strutting around telling everybody he had told them so.

I began reading the symptoms, the first of which was "may cause GI upset," and before I could get another symptom read, Pink interrupted.

"It did more than just upset them GIs. It killed a bunch of them!"

What would you have said to that? I just kinda giggled with the left half of my mouth and looked around to see how the rest of the crowd was reacting to that statement.

To my surprise, no one was reacting at all. They were just agreeing with Pink and waiting for the next symptom to be read. I sure wanted to break down laughing, but it is hard to do when no one else even got it. So, I just continued reading symptoms, and we all went to work to save the giant dog.

*twenty three*

## Travels

# Moment 1

### *Blue Minivan*

Every region has its own package of directional terms. I think every veterinarian should take the time to write down proper directions. If I were in charge of veterinary school curriculum, I would make Rural Navigation and Communications a required class for senior veterinary students.

Since becoming a veterinarian, I have been lost countless times. The problem usually lies in one overwhelming fact: the people who are giving the directions have lived in the area in question for years, and the person getting the directions has not.

Over the years, I have learned that the secret lies in a few key "do nots":

**1. Do not** write down any direction that has the word "before" in it. Here is an example: "You will turn left about a mile and a half before you get to an S-shaped curve in the road." Sounds crazy, but it has happened to me two or three times since I have become a direction receiver. You would think that I would have learned after the first mile-and-a-half trip back that "before" was not part of the direction receiver's vocabulary.

**2. Do not** write down any direction that has time as a unit of measure. Here is an example: The seventy-five-year-old rancher who comes to town only every other Monday tells you, "And then you'll go straight on that road for about ten minutes and turn back to the east." How far do you think that fella went in ten minutes? Three miles, four miles? At a mile a minute, it would be ten miles. Never in a hundred years would I have guessed it was one mile, but it was. That is right, he drives one mile in ten minutes. Wow! No wonder he comes to town only twice a month.

**3. Do not** write down any directions that have "relative" terms. Here is an example: "You will be on a paved road now. Stay on this road until you come to a dirt road with deep ditches. You will turn south there." I had to go back and forth on that road for what seemed like hours comparing the depth of ditches until I determined which one appeared to be the deepest. I was figuring when I wrote the directions down that there would be one road with deep ditches. Wrong. They all had deep ditches. This guy only noticed the one he always drives on.

**4. Do not** write down anything for a landmark that is not fixed to the earth. Here is an example: "After you turn here, you will go awhile until you come to a house with a blue minivan parked in the driveway. You will make a right there." Of course, the minivan was gone when I happened by. I drove about ten miles past the intended house before I finally gave up and went back.

There are a few other things worth mentioning. The only way that a place can be named after a person is if they are dead or have moved away. This further complicates learning the area for a newcomer. Here is an example: "You will drive south on this road until you come to the edge of the old Carlton place. You will turn east here." Come to find out that Mr. Carlton died in 1944 and has no living relatives.

Another thing worth mentioning is volume. If the directions have a repetition of more than five things in them as you encounter the landmark, jot a mark on your windshield. Here is an example: "After this, you will be on the ranch. You will go straight for quite a while, and then you will veer left after the twelfth cattle guard." Of course, you know that I lost count at seven and had to go back and start all over.

By far, the most important thing to do is get specifics. Things like barn color, house color, building materials used, county road numbers, exact measurements, mailboxes, telephone poles, and any natural landmarks will cut down on how much fun it is to drive through the countryside for half a day comparing ditch depth.

I've become so intent on getting good directions that I'm sure I get on some people's nerves. For example, I made one man describe every detail about his house and its surroundings, only to find when I got there that it was the only house for miles. Oh, and make sure you don't use time a element of measure or you may find out you can walk as far in ten minutes as some old ranchers drive.

# Moment 2

*Boxer Shorts*

I have always heard about hog operations in the Upper Midwest but had never actually been to one until recently. These places are the pinnacle of where science and agriculture meet. The pigs are genetically programmed to grow fast and efficiently while being resistant to many diseases. This disease resistance doesn't keep these hog farmers from being sticklers for cleanliness, though; oh no, they are germ nuts. That's right, they don't want even one germ to enter their pig facilities. This is where the story starts.

One of my hosts at this vet clinic in the Upper Midwest had been so kind as to arrange a tour of one of the farrowing facilities in his practice. I was looking forward to experiencing high-tech pig production at its finest. On the trip over, he explained the production expectations of such an operation: fifteen hundred sows in one building having litters 2.5 times per year and shooting to wean about twenty-six pigs per sow per year. Wow, that is making some pork. I was anxious to see how all this worked as we pulled into the farm.

As we entered the front door of the farrowing facility, I estimated the building to be about the size of a football field. It was quite, clean, odorless, and well kept. The first person we encountered as we entered the reception area was the owner of the facility. She was a kind-looking woman with a wonderful smile and an extreme Midwestern accent.

"Glad to see ya. You guys grab a shower and come on in," were her opening words from the "germ-free" area.

I had heard about this shower thing but had never actually done it. This is a requirement for anyone who enters one of these high-tech facilities. You have to take off all of your clothes, take a shower (including washing your hair), and on the other side of the shower, clothes to wear while you are in with the pigs will be provided for you.

The other vet went through, and a red light came on indicating that it was my turn. The first little room was separated from the second little room by a shower. I was to take off all of my clothes and take a shower. *No big deal*, I thought, *I'll just hang my clothes here and hop into this shower*. So I did.

The problem came when I entered the next little room on the other side of the shower. Here I was, totally naked, and there it was, a pile of underwear. Underwear is just one of those things that people don't share. I guess I had never been put in the situation of having to pick out a pair of underwear to put on that someone else had been wearing. What do you do? It kinda gave me the willies. And where exactly did these underwear come from? Were they left here by others? Did they go to Walmart and buy a variety pack? Sheesh.

I started considering what qualities I would like in a pair of underwear that had recently covered the fanny of a total stranger. After a moment of sorting, it became apparent that size was the major issue. Big, that's right, the bigger the better. In fact, so big that they actually touch nothing except the waist. And there they were, a pair of argyle boxers big enough for an offensive lineman for the Minnesota Vikings. Inspection of the tag in the band revealed a waist size of fifty-two.

I slid into them and then put on a pair of coveralls. The rest of my trip through the hog facility was spent listening with one ear while trying to keep the size-fifty-two boxers from sliding off. I kept one hand in my pocket, clutching that waistband, for as long as possible.

Finally, a situation arrived that required both of my hands. The boxers immediately fell down to the inseam of the also-oversized coveralls. There is no way to pull up a pair of size-fifty-two boxers once they have fallen without taking off the coveralls, so I decided to just leave them alone and make the best of it.

As far as I know, no one could tell it happened. The only effect it had on me was a great reduction in my stride length. I had to take about two steps to their one for the rest of the tour.

The moral of the story is this: if I ever go into another hog facility that requires showering, I will carry an extra pair of my own underwear that has been wrapped and autoclaved.

# Moment 3

*Cauliflower*

I arrived a bit late at the continuing-education meeting and stood at the door, trying to decide where to sit. After a busy workday, it's hard to make these evening meetings on time, especially when they're sixty miles away.

The crowd was already seated around tables, waiting for dinner to be served. I didn't know anyone, so I just chose the first open seat I came to, introduced myself to those at the table, and began evaluating them subconsciously, as we all are prone to do.

The meeting topic had attracted both city and rural veterinarians. I always enjoy these kinds of meetings because they bring together the wide variety of people and personalities who make up our profession.

The circular table seated twelve. To my left was a group from a rural veterinary practice—a vet and four techs, still wearing a bit of the day's aroma. To my right was another DVM, his wife, and four techs who obviously had spent their day inside, working on small animals.

Conversation was minimal. Groups like this have little in common and often sit on different sides of the veterinary fence.

The city-vet's wife seemed a bit abrasive. She was much overdressed for the occasion and seemed to look down her nose at the country vets. As luck would have it, she was immediately to my right; I, too, was a bit smelly after a long, hot day.

The arrival of dinner seemed to cut the tension a bit. We were served a chicken dish with steamed vegetables. The veggies would have been good if cooked properly, but these were a bit rubbery. There was broccoli, cauliflower, squash, and some other green thing that I couldn't identify.

The servers later came by to pour a glass of wine for those who wanted it. Most of us declined, but the ritzy wife asked them to leave the whole bottle. It didn't take her long to consume it, with a little help from her husband and a younger woman. The more the wife drank, the ruder she became. She went on about how great their clinic was and how smart her husband was.

Then she began praising the quality of the food as she chomped down on those steamed veggies. As I looked around the table, no one else had been able to cut even one piece into a bite small enough to eat.

The young woman to my left, from the country practice, seemed a bit shy. Her hands told a story of hard work, and she was not digging those vegetables. I watched her work on the cauliflower. It was so large and perfectly round that she couldn't figure a way to cut it. She tried the fork first. No luck. Then she tried stabbing it with the fork. Again, no luck. Finally, she held it with the fork and cut it with the knife.

This led to a remarkable event: when she pressed down with the knife, the rubbery cauliflower suddenly shot off her plate, bounced once in my lap, and came to rest somewhere deep within the ritzy wife's partly opened purse.

We just looked at each other with one-cornered smiles and kept listening to the now semidrunk, overdressed woman go on about something that made her look great and the rest of us look stupid. We never said a word.

That cauliflower was drenched in some high-viscosity sauce that left a stain on my trousers. I could just imagine what it must be doing to the contents of that high-dollar purse. I started to say something, but about that time, she looked at me and made some subliminally rude comment about my practice. I just smiled and nodded.

I wonder where she was when she found that cauliflower. I laughed about it all the way home. She left the room that night carrying a cauliflower the size of a baseball and most likely would blame me for it at some point.

Oh well.

# Moment 4

*Cop and Reindeer*

The roads of West Texas are painfully lonely at 2:00 a.m. In fact, I had not seen a car in twenty minutes as I sped toward a waiting reindeer.

Why does it seem that reindeer always go into labor at 2:00 a.m.?

There is one thing about being the only vehicle on the road—you are very noticeable. As I mounted the only hill in Gaines County, there was nothing else for the police officer to look at but a speeding veterinarian headed for a reindeer delivery.

*Great,* I thought. *There is no way this guy is going to believe me.*

He ambled up to the truck with that typical "cautious policeman" gait. I could feel the beam of his flashlight bouncing off of my head as I anticipated his smirk when I informed him of my mission.

"Could I see your driver's license, please, sir?"

"Well, Mr. Brock, any reason you are in such a hurry at this late hour?"

I always feel like a third-grader who has been sent to the principal's office when the law pulls me over. As much as I wanted to sound convincing, I just choked up on the next few words that came out of my mouth. The noise that poured forth sounded like a fourteen-year-old boy who was going through the "yodel" that comes with puberty.

"Um, yes, Officer, I was just on my way to deliver a reindeer baby."

If I had not been in such a hurry, the look that came over his face would have been something to let hang in the air for a while and savor. But with the urgency of the matter, I decided to expound a bit more.

"You see, I am a veterinarian, and there is a female reindeer about five miles down the road that is having a critical time delivering; she's having a dystocia."

I decided to throw in the big word there at the end to perhaps add a bit of credibility to my claim. It was not until this moment in my veterinary history that I realized that there was no way to prove that I actually am a veterinarian!

"You mean to tell me that you are speeding though the warm, West Texas night to deliver a baby reindeer? Well, I've heard it all now," came bubbling from his lips behind an expression that joined a slight grin with a look of disgust.

"Listen, my friend, this reindeer is worth about ten thousand bucks if I can get it out before it dies. I know you are here to enforce the law, so if you are going to give me a ticket, would you mind following me over to the reindeer and writing it out as I bring that critter into the world?"

My pubescent voice had turned to an incredibly authoritative one with absolutely no conscious effort. In fact, I was hoping that I had not sounded too bossy when some bass finally came back to my tones.

Much to my surprise, the officer suddenly became excited and urgent himself. He almost panicked. He began shuffling his feet and folding the papers that filled his hands. He looked down the road as if to visualize this reindeer going through the Lamaze steps in anticipation of her doctor arriving.

"I just don't believe anyone could make something like that up," he said. "You just run along now and save that baby's life."

"Good luck," was the last thing I heard him say as I pulled back onto the road to finish my calling.

I got there in plenty of time to help ol' Rudolph take his first breath. I've often wondered if the police officer went back to the station and told his buddies, or if he just kept it to himself, figuring they would all make fun of him and think he was crazy. I've also wondered if it would work every time.

# *twenty four*
## Final Thoughts

# Moment 1

*Pathology and Spiders*

I sat there looking at that computer screen, thinking, *How in the world can this thing be full?* The worst of all nightmares had struck Brock Veterinary Clinic, and during the process of trying to repair the damage, the screen came up with a message telling me that my memory was full. Boy, did this complete an already disastrous problem!

I sat in the third row, watching a herd of three- and four-year-old children sing songs under the perfect orchestration of Ms. Young. I couldn't help but admire her infinite patience and gift of gab with little kids. The third song in the second set flooded my brain with thoughts of being a child and this concept of full memories.

⊱⋅⊰

I sat in my study chair on the second floor of a rented duplex in Bryan, Texas, in 1987, studying for the last final of my sophomore year of veterinary school. Things were just not clicking. If you have ever gone through one of those marathon study sessions, then you know the feeling. I was studying for my seventh comprehensive final in as many days. To make matters worse, the subject was pathology. Man, it was dry.

You might be wondering what computers, singing children, and second-year pathology have in common. Let's go back to that night in May 1987, and I'll see if I can put it all together.

Kerri's voice snapped me from a too-much-studying daze as she opened the door to the upstairs room. "Why in the world are you singing that song?" she asked as I returned to a conscious state.

"I don't know," I gurgled from my mouth as I pondered the question myself.

"You have lost your mind. It is a good thing you are almost through with finals; I think your brain is full," she said as she turned and left the room.

The more I pondered it, the more I thought this jesting phrase that she left me with might be true. I had not thought of that song in years. In fact, it had not entered my mind since I was a little bitty boy. Why in the world did I start singing it in the middle of studying about infarcts? I was beginning to think that my brain was full, and it had started looking around for information that had not been used in years to move to the recycle bin.

I ran down the steps and told Kerri my theory. She just gave me a look that said I'd confirmed her suspicion: I had lost my mind. She told me she was going to bed.

Back up the stairs I trod and somehow found room to shove the rest of the infarct story into my brain, which I now concluded had enough room to hold the rest of my second-semester pathology.

This sudden ejection of useless memories had happened to me several times over the course of veterinary school, but none of the experiences was as vivid as the first. I was convinced that my brain would hold only so much, and that it had become full that night in May.

∽≪৯

The third song of the set was "The Itsy Bitsy Spider," and this was the very song that had oozed helplessly out of my head that night in Bryan. As I heard twenty kids sing it aloud, all of the information about infarcts that I had stored on my hard drive trickled out of my brain and bounced across the floor of the gym at the First Baptist Church.

If you ever show up at the Brock Veterinary Clinic with an animal and find me suddenly breaking out in the "The Itsy Bitsy Spider," then you can feel sure that your animal has an infarct. I've determined that "The Itsy Bitsy Spider" is much more fun than pathology.

# Moment 2

### *Pucker*

I grew up watching my grandmother quilt. She sewed every evening. I would watch her and think how cool it looked for her to slip that needle through the cloth with the aid of a thimble or two. She would tell me that I needed to be practicing on cloth so I would be ready for skin when I became a veterinarian. So, I would help her put a "blind hem" stitch in the patterns of the quilt. I did it for hours in the evenings as I grew up. She made it look so easy; all the pieces were precut and fit together so well. I figured that the only difference would be that sewing is on cloth, and suturing is on tissue, but I was on track for an education.

Soon after becoming an animal surgeon, I realized that tissue seldom goes together as nicely as precut patterns do. If you are doing an elective surgery, such as a spay or neuter, then sure, the skin edges go back together just like the patterns on those quilts. But if you are repairing a horse that ran through a fence, or the leftovers of a dogfight, then typically the parts just don't fit.

To get an idea of what I mean, cut a circle in a paper towel and see if you can sew the thing back together; or better yet, try attaching a garden hose to an inner tube.

The end result of suturing things back together that don't fit is a pucker. Over the years, I have faced them countless times. When one side is longer than the other is, a pucker results as you approach the end of the cut. The question is what do you do with a pucker?

It just sticks out, begging for some attention. Most of the time, the owner is standing there, peering over my shoulder with that look on his face that expresses a complete lack of confidence.

I've even had people ask me, "What in the world are you going to do with that *great big pucker* that is forming as you go?"

I have overcome my fear of puckers in the last year or so. We have developed a five-step approach to handling them. If there is someone in the room with you, say the next sentence aloud for full appreciation of its melody.

"You can poke a pucker, tuck a pucker, pleat a pucker, dart a pucker, or cut a pucker. We go through this series of remedies, and we quit when one works."

We start by poking the pucker with one of our suturing instruments. It will disappear beneath adjacent skin, and if it doesn't leave too big of a bump or come out when you shake it, then you are done.

If the bump is too big or the pucker bulges when you shake it, then you should try to tuck the pucker by putting a stitch over it to hold it underneath the surrounding skin. If it works without leaving too much of an ugly pile of skin, then you are done.

If the pucker tucking is unsuccessful, then go to the pleat technique. Simply take one big pucker and make a bunch of little puckers out of it. They're a little like pleated pants: They lie flat but have room to expand. This works well and can be quite cosmetic. If it works, then quit; you are done.

But some puckers are too stubborn even for the pleat technique. These require the assistance of scissors. The pucker should be grasped with a pair of forceps while you remove a neat wedge of skin. The *V* that is left in the skin then can be sutured together to form a nice, neat *I*. All but the most treacherous of puckers can be defeated by this dart-a-pucker procedure.

The frustration level might be a tad high if this procedure doesn't work, so we come to the last resort: cut a pucker. Grab the thing; cut it off, and walk away before your blood pressure gets any higher. I would not recommend this technique in front of squeamish clients.

Oh, I forgot to mention what is perhaps my favorite variety of pucker. Our girls call it the plant-a-pucker; it's what Kerri and I put on their rosy cheeks every night as we tuck them into bed.

# Moment 3

## *Tough Crowd*

I was talking to a client today, and it occurred to me that my job often requires telling folks things they don't want to hear—bad news about a disease, tough love about diets for fat pets, problems that we have no cure for, or prices for procedures that may exceed their budgets. The list goes on and on. To top this off, I really never know how they are going to take the news or what their response may be.

I have been blessed beyond what I deserve in many areas of life. I have given funny, motivational, and informative talks all over this country and overseas. I remember many of them with fondness and smiles and very seldom find myself terrified of the group before me. But on one particular occasion, I was terrified of the group before me.

A friend had asked me to give a funny talk to a group on a date close to Christmas. I owed this woman a favor and said I would be glad to give a talk. The one thing I failed to ask was who this group of people might be. I wrote the date on my calendar and promptly forgot all about it. The months passed, and as the week approached, she called to remind me and give me a location.

I arrived at the location and was surprised that it was next to a hospital and that it didn't appear to be a meeting hall. I walked into a reception area and told the receptionist that I had been given directions to this location to give a talk. She smiled graciously and shook my hand. She led me through a series of hallways into an office, where I was instructed to wait. She told me that my friend would soon arrive.

I had my computer containing all of the usual funny animal slides. I was going through my talk in my head as my friend walked into the office. She gave me a big hug and thanked me profusely for coming to talk to this group. She said they sure needed a lift and something to laugh about during the holidays.

My curiosity began to rise when she said they sure needed a lift around the holidays. I thanked her for asking me and then gingerly asked, "Who, exactly, am I talking to?"

"You mean you don't know?" she asked, her eyebrows high on her forehead.

I was beginning to scroll through my brain, wondering why I didn't know something that seemed so obvious to her. I was beginning to feel a little pressure and wasn't sure why.

"These people are all terminally ill. I have heard you give talks many times and believe you will make them laugh and be happy."

*What?* How did I miss this detail? My brain suddenly became mush as I considered the task. What in the world could I possibly say to dying people at Christmas that could make them happy?

"I absolutely had no idea this would be the audience! I am not even kinda prepared to do this. I was just gonna give a talk about the life of a veterinarian and all the funny things we see every day. These people ain't gonna want to hear that stuff!"

The pitch of my voice and the sweat forming on my face clued her in to my panic. "Don't worry. I have heard that talk before. They will love it," she said in a calm tone that made me want to strangle her.

She led me down yet another hall, through a large double door, and into a conference room. This was no normal conference room; it had perhaps 150 hospital beds and soft chairs in it, and in those beds and chairs were people who fit the bill of exactly whom she said I would be addressing.

She seated me on a stage next to a podium, and before I even had a moment to persuade my brain that everything would be OK, an AV dude had my computer hooked up, and she had introduced me.

I stood up behind that podium and looked out over the crowd. Those folks did not look like they were in any mood to laugh. Do you know how hard it is to tell stories that are supposed to be funny to people who don't laugh? It is awful. I had maybe fifteen stories to get through, and I was filled with dread. I could feel cold sweat dripping from every sweat-producing gland my body possessed. I must have stood there for a good fifteen seconds without uttering a word.

Finally, I found the courage to begin. Some lower level of my brain must have convinced an upper level of my brain that my talk would never be over if I didn't get started.

I went through the first story, laying it out with all the gusto I could muster. When the point of the story that should invoke laughter arrived, I heard not a peep.

It was my best story. If they didn't laugh at that, I might as well just get off that stage and head back to Lamesa. I was petrified. Five seconds, ten seconds, maybe headed to fifteen seconds and still there was not even a peep.

Just about the time I was ready to pack it in, an old dude in a wheel-chair to my left began to cackle in a gruff, raspy roll. This prompted a woman in the fourth row, lying in a bed and wearing one of those hospital gowns that make you feel more naked than if you were actually naked, start laughing loud and hard. The giggles spread, and soon the entire room was leg-slapping happy.

I couldn't believe it. These dying and depressed people were crack-ing up. Tears were running down faces that looked as though they hadn't smiled in years. I paused for a long moment to absorb what had just happened. The story is pretty funny, but it had never made anyone laugh like that.

They just kept laughing and talking to one another about similar things that had happened in their lives.

I probably talked for two hours. We had the best time. I went out into the audience as I spoke and got them involved in the stories. They thanked me a thousand times for coming, and I must have gotten a sloppy cheek kiss from half the audience.

As I was talking to that client today, I remembered that evening with the people I thought would never laugh. You just never know by looking who might be dying for a reason to smile.

# Moment 4

## *Lab Test*

Labs. That was what they called those scheduled classes in veterinary school in which they taught us to do the stuff we were gonna do in real life when we got out. We all liked these things called labs because it got us out of the classroom for a while and reminded us of why we came to vet school in the first place.

We had all kinds of these labs; we learned how to float teeth on a horse, how to put intravenous catheters in dogs, and how to palpate cows. One lab was just amazing.

I entered the basement of the vet school with my lab partner and best friend, John Horn. We were always on time for everything, but for some reason on that day, we were a bit late. We always read our lab the prior day to be ready for it, but for some reason, we had not done that either.

When I rounded the corner and entered the room that this particular event was occurring in, I could not believe what my eyes beheld. At first I was dumbfounded, and then I began to giggle, and finally I was mortified. This was a lab for collecting semen from a dog. I personally had never considered how one gets semen out of a dog. I had done it in bulls and stallions, but never even thought about doing it in a dog.

Remember, I said that at first I was dumbfounded. I had known the people in my class for two and a half years. There were 128 of us, and after spending forty or fifty hours a week together for that long, you knew everything about everyone. You may wonder why dumbfounded would be a proper first emotion. Well, I will tell you why. It seemed that the only way to get semen out of a dog was the old-fashioned way—by hand. Holy mackerel!

Here I was, entering a room with my buddy, John, only to find a tableful of girls from my class whom I had known for two and a half years, doing *that* to a dog.

Now remember, neither one of us had read the lab, so we had no idea what was going on. The girls at the first table we encountered were a group of very proper women in our class. I never even considered that they would even know how to do something like that. Yet, there they were, just getting after it on that dog.

That led to the second emotion I described earlier—I began to giggle. To see the very prim and proper vet students doing that to a dog just hit me funny. And it hit John the same way at about the same time, because I could hear his familiar snicker developing as I felt my face turning red. These gals were working it. They were all ugly in the face, trying to get this twenty-five-pound mutt to give them a semen sample so they could evaluate it under the microscope set up at the same table.

Now, I realize that we were in professional school, and things like that shouldn't have been funny. But watching four proper vet students doing that to a dog was frickin' funny. I didn't care if they were wearing white lab coats while they did it; it did not look professional to me at all, and it just made me laugh. And I didn't want to laugh too loudly, so I was suppressing my laughter, which led to those occasional small outbursts of giggles followed by a recomposure.

But the funny wasn't over. My glance moved to the next table past the door, only to find four country-boy redneck-type fellas doing the same thing. Horn saw them about the same time I did, and he nudged my shoulder and pointed.

There was definitely a different look on these faces. One guy manned the pole and the other three stood there red-faced and disgusted. They were wearing rubber gloves and palpation sleeves and had their sunglasses on, as if maybe no one would recognize them. Horn was laughing aloud now, and this opened the door for me to let it go and laugh hard with him. These guys had a forty-five-pound blue heeler, and that dog was smiling like there was no tomorrow.

Remember I told you there were three emotions? Well, suddenly I entered the third emotion, *mortified*, because I realized that I was going to have to do that same thing. Eeeeesh.

John Horn quit laughing about the same time that I did as a woman from the back entered the lab with an old-looking beagle dog and handed the leash to me. She informed me that we would be sorry we were late because we'd gotten the last dog, Snoopy, and he was a fifteen-year-old beagle that had been through this lab about thirty times and knew how to make it last. (Did she just say, "make it last"?) She said that he had only two responsibilities in this world; one was donating blood, and the other was this lab. She went on to say that he liked this responsibility much more than being an occasional blood donor.

As I continued to look around the room for an empty table, I noticed that some people were already through and looking at the collected samples. Their dogs were gone, and they were about done and ready to go home. Man, we were just five minutes late; those dogs must have been easy collections. Our dog, on the other hand, looked like he was no adolescent rookie. He was giving John a romantic look and sort of pacing his gait as we walked toward the table.

"I will get the dog on the table and get the microscope ready. You can do the stroking," came bubbling out of my mouth as I picked old Snoopy up and set him on the table.

"No way, dude! I will get the microscope ready; you ain't getting off that easy!" John replied as he wrestled the dog out of my arms and set him closer to my side.

"Maybe we can talk one of those girls at the first table into coming to get the sample. They looked like they were really good at it. Why don't you go ask them, and I will hold the dog?" I asked him while he stared at the rubber glove I had tossed to him.

"No way, dude! I am not asking a woman to do that. I think you should just do it and get it over with," John replied.

"OK. Let's just flip a coin and get done with this so we can go home," I said.

Of course, I lost the toss. Arrrgh! I couldn't believe I had to do this to a fifteen-year-old beagle. And by now, everyone else was through, but they weren't leaving. No, they had seen me laugh at them, and now it was their turn to get me back. Not only that, but I had the Romeo of the dog world, and the woman had told me already that he knew how to make it last.

I went to work. I didn't even have any sunglasses. This dog was the master. He would almost deliver, and then it was as if he realized it and relaxed all over, so I would have to start again. Everyone in the general area was laughing hysterically, and I was about as embarrassed as I had ever been in my life. Even the woman who had brought Snoopy out was standing across the room watching. I could tell she had seen Snoopy operate many times before and was giggling at my misfortune. I couldn't help but think that if we were anywhere but in veterinary school, I would go to jail for doing this to a dog.

That lab finally came to an end after what seemed like an hour, and with it came my resolution that I would *never* do that again. If my clients ever needed a semen evaluation on their dogs, they were just gonna have to do that themselves, because I was absolutely never going to do that again.

*twenty five*

## Leonard

# Leonard

I had worked on Leonard's horses since they were eight years old. Now, as I approached the two geldings from across a field of West Texas clover, they were twenty-eight. Leonard was a crusty old codger who'd been a cowboy in Borden County for seventy-five years—it was all he'd ever known. His wife had died the previous September after they'd spent fifty-five years together, raising cattle and living off the land. Their ranch house they spent their lives in got water from a windmill and electricity from the sun and wind. Their lives were as fulfilling as any I'd ever seen.

This trip across the clover to catch the two old horses was bringing tears to my eyes. These geldings had spent their lives serving Leonard and his wife, and they both had worn out at the same time. It was time for them to be put to sleep.

Leonard had stayed back at the barn. He had his arms draped over the top rail of a pipe fence and his hat pulled down over his eyes so we couldn't see the tears streaming down his cheeks.

Dr. Emily Berryhill had come with me to the ranch. She was the intern at our clinic and hadn't been around long enough to know the history of Leonard, so I filled her in as we ambled across the field to catch the horses. I looked over and saw tears in her eyes. Emily hadn't seen this side of the gruff cowboys who come to our clinic—the side that cries when his favorite horse is at the end of its life. She was now experiencing it firsthand.

Leonard had arranged for a neighbor to dig a hole under the only tree visible for miles. The plot was the perfect place for these two old geldings to be buried—it was their favorite spot to spend the day. From it, they could see their barn and get back to it in a hurry, if need be.

They could watch the cars pass on the county road in the distance. They could see the cliffs of the canyon to the west and watch the hawks ride the updrafts. These two critters loved to be in the shade of that tree, and that's where Leonard wanted them buried.

It's an awful job, killing a man's best friend. All of the memories of rounding up cattle and the stories of how those horses had gotten Leonard out of tough spots filled my mind as we laid the second one to rest in that hole. My trip back across the clover field to say good-bye to Leonard was a long one. I dreaded seeing his wrinkled eyes filled with the memories of how much he loved his horses.

We came through the last gate and hung the halters on their hook in the barn. I patted Leonard on the back and told him it broke my heart for him to have to say good-bye to them but assured him that it had been the right thing to do.

He looked up from under his hat, and the emotion of twenty-eight years of friendship ending on that day poured down his weathered cheeks.

"I'll be to town in a couple of days, and I'll get you paid, Doc," he told me. "Thanks for coming out here and doing that."

"You owe me nothing, Leonard. I couldn't live with myself if I charged a man to kill his best friend."

"But you drove seventy-five miles to get here, Doc," he said. "I gotta pay you som'in'."

I paused and thought a bit. Experiences like this one are why I dreamed of being a veterinarian when I was a kid. I get to work with the salt of the earth, people who understand the bond between people and animals. It's the essence of what veterinarians do, and it has nothing to do with state-of-the-art equipment or making money. I kept those horses happy and going for most of their lives, and I was a part of laying them to rest when their days were done.

Leonard appreciated that. He knew that taking care of critters from start to finish was simply what the local veterinarian did.

"You've been paying me for twenty years, my friend," I said. "This one is on me."

CPSIA information can be obtained at www.ICGtesting.com
Printed in the USA
LVOW04s1003110515

437909LV00038B/511/P